The Ethics of Doing Nothing

The Ethics of Doing Nothing

Rest, Rituals, and the Modern World

ANDREW BLOSSER

ORBIS BOOKS
Maryknoll, New York 10545

Founded in 1970, Orbis Books endeavors to publish works that enlighten the mind, nourish the spirit, and challenge the conscience. The publishing arm of the Maryknoll Fathers and Brothers, Orbis seeks to explore the global dimensions of the Christian faith and mission, to invite dialogue with diverse cultures and religious traditions, and to serve the cause of reconciliation and peace. The books published reflect the views of their authors and do not represent the official position of the Maryknoll Society. To learn more about Maryknoll and Orbis Books, please visit our website at www.orbisbooks.com.

All scripture quotations are taken from the translation of the New American Bible, Revised Edition (NABRE), used by permission.

Manufactured in the United States of America.
Manuscript editing and typesetting by Joan Weber Laflamme.

Library of Congress Cataloging-in-Publication Data

Names: Blosser, Andrew, author.
Title: The ethics of doing nothing : rest, rituals, and the modern world / Andrew Blosser.
Description: Maryknoll, New York : Orbis Books, [2023] | Includes biblio- graphical references and index. | Summary: "Addresses the obsession with material production by proposing 'rituals of inoperativity' such as Sabbath-keeping, vigils, and fiestas to 'change our understanding of what it means to be human.'"— Provided by publisher.
Identifiers: LCCN 2022035003 (print) | LCCN 2022035004 (ebook) | ISBN 9781626985025 (trade paperback) | ISBN 9781608339648 (epub)
Subjects: LCSH: Rest—Religious aspects—Catholic Church. | Work ethic.
Classification: LCC BV4597.55 B56 2022 (print) | LCC BV4597.55 (ebook) | DDC 241/.65—dc23/eng/20220907
LC record available at https://lccn.loc.gov/2022035003
LC ebook record available at https://lccn.loc.gov/2022035004

Dedicated to Kelvin Krantz
For whom hard work, leisure, and the beauty of humor
always coalesced.

Contents

Introduction

Justifying an Odd Investigation

What Is the Value of Doing Nothing?

The above question is not often contemplated by most politicians, scientists, businesspersons, activists, or even philosophers. Largely, the modern world consists of a summons to *do*—to make, invent, restore, and alter. We want to earn new degrees, go places, and find ways of being more productive in our jobs. When we are not actively working at our careers, we strive for self-improvement through physical exercise, mental cultivation, hobbies, and family investment. We dread gaps in activity, such as periods of unemployment, cancelled dates, or long lines at the amusement park. Younger generations chafe with a type of anxiety often given the acronym FOMO (fear of missing out). Our lives our consumed with kinetic and spiritual forward momentum.

Of course, doing is good. "Six days you may labor and do all your work," the Pentateuch says (Ex 20:9). The ancient Jewish sage Qoheleth concurs: "Whatever your hand finds to do, do it with all your strength" (Eccl 9:10). Disciplined, focused action has brought us tremendous benefits in the modern world. The industrial revolution—notwithstanding its pollutions and oppressions—created efficient technologies, scientific advancements, and medical wonders that have made living in the twenty-first century a relative luxury for many of earth's inhabitants. The prolific researcher and statistician

Steven Pinker has shown that by almost every metric of health and socioeconomic security, the current time in earth's history is the most comfortable for the greatest number of people.[1] A few simple contrasts establish this point beyond doubt. No more than two centuries ago, a toothache could be a death sentence; today, it requires only ibuprofen and a quick trip to the dentist. In the 1800s, wash day for a medium-sized family meant literally an entire working day devoted to hand-scrubbing laundry with skin-blistering soap; currently, machines wash our clothes for us while we do other things. A trip from New York to California in the 1820s for most Americans would have been a risky, months-long journey costing someone's life savings; today it can happen in a few hours for the price of a cheap sofa. Occasional Luddites and other nostalgic rustics may complain of the woes of a hyper-technologized society, but few truly want to return to a romantic hunter/gatherer or Stone Age agrarian existence. Camping, we say, is fun only because we do not have to do it all the time.

Also, our constant activity shows no signs of stopping, and it is continually improving our lives. Even setbacks such as the COVID-19 pandemic may serve as springboards for scientific advancements, such as rapid production of effective vaccines. Agricultural technologies have made farming easier, with less land use than ever before. Genetic engineering holds promise of ending some of the most vexing medical problems human beings face, even the most inevitable ones such as natural aging. In the realm of industry, Henry Ford's assembly-line efficiency was only the beginning; factories today are simultaneously speedier and less (physically) dangerous than ever before (though perhaps not less psychologically dangerous), and we have not yet reached our industrial productivity ceiling. The lesson of the last five hundred years seems to be, work, work, and keep working!

---

[1] See, for example, Steven Pinker, *Enlightenment Now: The Case for Reason, Science, Humanism, and Progress* (New York: Viking, 2018).

Nevertheless, all these accomplishments zealous work has created return us to the initial question, phrased differently: What do we do when all our work is done? What happens when human beings become inoperative? This may not seem like an imminent possibility, and it probably is not for most people. It is also possible that the amount of work to do in the universe is practically endless. Human beings will always face challenges that require labor and ingenuity. Technology is labor saving, but with every increase in technology more education is needed to shore up the workforce for maintaining the labor-saving technology, which means more work as well. But if we describe our work as progress (as most inventors and activists do), we must ask to what we are progressing. Furthermore, if the end goal of technology and industry is efficiency, this must mean that the total amount of human labor being performed will go down over time (unless technological innovation is a giant industrial treadmill, which would be a depressing thought to most innovators). As it turns out, this seems to be the case in some sectors of the so-called Western world. Research by Mark Aguiar and Erik Hurst shows that from 1965 to 2003, the amount of average leisure time Americans had access to increased dramatically, almost by a full working day.[2] A nostalgic cynic might argue that this is a result of increasing laziness and resulting poverty, but statistics indicate that the poverty rate in the United States has actually fallen substantially during that time, so a supposed "moral decline" in diligence cannot be an explanation.[3] It may be that human efficiency is truly resulting in less work to be done, leaving us more time to amuse ourselves.

---

[2] See Mark Aguiar and Erik Hurst, "Measuring Trends in Leisure: The Allocation of Time over Five Decades," NBER Working Paper Series (Cambridge, MA: National Bureau of Economic Research, 2006).

[3] For a handy overview of these trends in census data, see Dylan Matthews, "Poverty in the 50 Years since 'The Other America' in Five Charts," *Washington Post,* July 11, 2012.

The strange possibility of human beings running out of necessary work also lies behind recent politicians' calls for a universal basic income (UBI). During the 2020 presidential election, businessman Andrew Yang became famous for arguing that increasing use of automation in factories, transportation, and even healthcare would render so many jobs obsolete that a publicly funded universal wage would become essential. Research by the Brookings Institution backs up his claims somewhat, demonstrating that numerous jobs have (and likely will be) affected by the rise of robots.[4] Although the era of self-driving trucks and computer-conducted surgeries may be far off, the possibility is no longer pure science fiction. If such an economy does hypothetically emerge, what should those people do who cannot find a materially useful role for themselves? What value would their existence have?

You Can Rest . . . But Not!

Here we reach a paradox. If the future prospect of millions of human beings standing around twiddling their thumbs with nothing to do sounds absurd, there is ample reason why. Despite our access to increasing levels of leisure time, Westerners do not feel constantly rested and refreshed. It is quite the opposite. We feel burned out, stressed, and pushed to our limits. In her intriguing research on contemporary work habits, journalist Brigitte Schulte calls our collective feeling "the overwhelm."[5] She interviews an assortment of sociologists, economists, and philosophers who have puzzled over this feeling. If we actually

---

[4] The Brookings Institution conference, "Automation, Labor Market Institutions, and the Middle Class," December 12, 2019. For an overview of research papers presented, see https://www.brookings.edu/blog/up-front/2020/01/14/automation-and-labor-market-institutions/.

[5] See Brigitte Schulte, *Overwhelmed: Work, Love, and Play When No One Has the Time* (New York: Farrar, Straus and Giroux, 2014).

have extra time on our hands (as the statistics clearly show), why do we feel so busy?

One cynical answer is that we truly are not very busy at all but simply wish to look like we are. Being harried can—at least in some circumstances—be a status symbol in a capitalist society where no one wants to appear slothful. Nevertheless, Schulte and most researchers handily reject this easy answer. Most of us truly feel overwhelmed—the evidence from therapists, anonymous surveys, and popular life experiences is just too, well, overwhelming. Furthermore, if anything, lavish vacations and relaxing getaways are just as much a sign of status as long days in the office. Some of the most prominent influencers in the modern world acquire their status from using social media to give the impression that they perpetually relax at the edge of infinity pools in tropical paradises. I personally know some people who will take hundreds of photos while on a once-a-year vacation and then purposefully post them on Instagram sporadically throughout the year to make it appear that they take more leisure trips than they really do.

There are two more convincing explanations for why we feel overworked and constantly busy. The first is that our apparent access to leisure time is illusory—we are not really resting when we think we are. The upside of modern technology is that it makes our work more accessible than ever, but its downside is that it also makes it sometimes impossible to escape. When the COVID-19 pandemic struck the United States, numerous workers found themselves virtual commuting from their bedrooms, which seemed delightful until they realized that this new arrangement made them de facto constantly available to bosses, managers, and clients. This problem can be compounded by the fact that often the most stressful and exhausting aspect of work is not the labor itself but the anxiety from being constantly under pressure to perform, or not knowing whether your job is secure. As many medical professionals know firsthand, lying in bed while being on call is not nearly as relaxing as lying in it with no potential obligations.

The second reason we may feel overwhelmed is also the pernicious flipside of an otherwise positive modern phenomenon: We feel as if our career possibilities are endless, and thus our work drive can never be satisfied. We must create work to do, not because we *have to* but because we *can*.

Alain de Botton claims that modern self-help literature and motivational rhetoric have set us up for this weird phenomenon. Prior to the arrival of industrial democracy in Europe and America, de Botton argues, class stratification enabled people to accept their lot in life. If you were a pauper, you stayed a pauper no matter how hard you worked. De Botton notes:

> The rigid hierarchy that had been in place in almost every Western society until the late eighteenth century, denying all hope of social movement except in the rarest of cases, the system glorified by John of Salisbury and John Fortescue, was unjust in a thousand all too obvious ways, but it offered those on the lowest rungs one notable freedom: the freedom not to have to take the achievements of quite so many people in society as reference points—and so find themselves severely wanting in status and importance as a result.[6]

Toward the end of the 1700s, official class rigidities began to relax, even as the forces that kept classes in place continued. Although for most people being born into poverty meant staying in poverty, it became theoretically possible to rise through the economic ranks with a smidgeon of diligence and a platterful of luck. Consequently, writers such as Benjamin Franklin inaugurated the "rags to riches" genre of literature, one continued in the present day by voices such as Tony Robbins and Ben

---

[6] Alain de Botton, *Status Anxiety* (New York: Random House, 2004), 35.

Carson. Popular phrases such as "you can do anything you put your mind to," "with enough hard work, anyone can succeed," or de Botton's favorite, "we all have the capability to carry out our dreams," lead us to think that if we have not created the perfect career, the fault is ours.

A careful investigation of these widely accepted phrases reveals them to be manifestly absurd. Not everyone can win the gold medal in the Olympics, write a book on the *New York Times* bestseller list, play in the NBA, or win a teacher-of-the-year award (there are way too many teachers and too few years). But somehow we believe them anyway. And if we believe deep down that we hold the capacity to accomplish anything, career inadequacy becomes an unbearable load of shame. If an aspiring actor believes he has the talent for Broadway and he does not get a role after a decade of auditioning, there is no one else to blame but him. A bodybuilder who thinks that she can win a Ms. Olympia if she trains diligently enough will be crushed when she loses, because she thinks she could have won if she tried harder. A parent who believes his focused nurturing can produce a prodigious, successful child will face a crisis when the child drops out of school. De Botton concludes that "the price we have paid for expecting to be so much more than our ancestors is a perpetual anxiety that we are far from being all we might be."[7] The terror lurking in the modern career is not that we are unable to do what we want, but that theoretically we can.

The result of our sense of limitless possibilities through work is that we feel compelled to never cease working, or at least worrying about working. Our brains are addled by a toxic drive constantly to thrust ourselves at perfection. We view contentment as laziness, and thus discontent rules our lives, directing us to always work harder and longer—regardless of whether our work is truly needed.

---

[7] De Botton, 44.

In our more reflective moments we may sense that we are working too much, and so we schedule time off. But the mirage of indefinite success hangs over us even when we try to relax. In a cruel twist, even our forms of relaxation are subject to the success drive. The aforementioned influencers have persuaded us that our vacations must have certain status symbols associated with them. We must go to the best resorts, see the most beautiful sights, and drink the finest beverages. We must only go to the beach if we have svelte abdominals, and if we go on a skiing trip we must buy a luxurious parka. Our holiday dinners require idealized features that necessitate days of backbreaking kitchen labor. Holidays themselves have become work. A friend of mine revealed to me that even video gamers feel status anxiety when they compare their recreational feats to those of elite players.

The modern person is therefore overworked not always because of the material necessities of life, but because the modern paradigm has identified human nature with work. The upshot is that the thought of doing nothing terrifies us. An inoperative person is literally worthless. Historian Richard Donkin points out that the modern career-minded person has learned never to challenge the necessity of work: "Suggesting that we might enjoy more leisure time, or asking 'Why do we work?' is looked upon with scorn and suspicion, as the language of the shirker."[8] Expanding on Max Weber's thesis, Donkin argues that this mentality emerges from a framework in which work is a sacred way of being—and its opposite is therefore sin. I would argue that in many cases, the situation is far more intense. In the prevailing paradigm, work is the only way for humans to establish their humanity, to confer existence upon themselves. The modern career is therefore a treadmill poised above an abyss. To step off it is to enter a void of unmeaning

---

[8] Richard Donkin, *The History of Work* (London: Palgrave Macmillan, 2010), xx.

so terrifying as to boggle the imagination. And if that does not scare you, there is yet another outcome that might.

And Now We Have Become the Destroyer of Worlds

Everything I have described thus far may sound to you like so much "yuppie kvetching," as Elizabeth Kolbert calls it.[9] We are too busy, we have no time, we are miserable, we need a break, and so on. The most austere among us might tell us to "suck it up" and be glad we have jobs to do.

However, there is a much more lethal crisis looming behind the modern compulsion to never stop working: climate change. As the scientific community repeatedly warns us, this is no minor problem on the stage of earth's history. A recent report by the United Nations soberly reminds us that global warming may reverse many of the advances in health and living standards reached by developing countries over the past century, as well as introducing new ones.[10] Although the effects of climate change seem less severe in temperate regions of the globe, desertification and atmospheric upheaval in equatorial regions may lead to exacerbating economic inequality worldwide, leading to increases in migration and potential violence.[11] And researchers at the World Bank warn that climate change could shove an extra 100 million people below the poverty line by 2030.[12] Truly this is no slight hiccup in the majestic drama of human progress.

---

[9] Elizabeth Kolbert, "No Time: How Did We Get So Busy," *New Yorker*, May 19, 2020.

[10] See Paritosh Kasotia, "The Health Effects of Global Warming: Developing Countries Are the Most Vulnerable," *The United Nations Chronicle* 44, no. 2, "Green Our World!" (June 2007).

[11] See UN Press Release, "Unprecedented Impacts of Climate Change Disproportionately Burdening Developing Countries, Delegate Stresses, as Second Committee Concludes General Debate," GA/EF/3516, October 8, 2019.

[12] See World Bank, "Climate Change: Overview," updated April 8, 2022.

The causes of climate change are complex, but they all eventually lead back to human activity or work. It is tempting to think that global warming is a problem caused by a few vicious industrialists—the coal-mining system, manufacturing, and meat production. In a sense this is true. But we are all part of an interwoven fabric of human cooperation, and all the activities of these nefarious actors are—in no metaphorical sense—our own. Whether we fall on the political left or the right, we elect politicians who promise to boost growth, which means doing more work, which invariably means emitting more greenhouse gases. James Carville's 1992 quip, "It's the economy, stupid," is both an electioneering slogan and a factual explanation for the causes of climate change. The planet heats up because we do not want to cease working.

The roots of climate change in our robust sense of diligence are also part of the reason why coming up with solutions to the climate crisis is so difficult. Our brains are wired to think that if certain people are causing disastrous problems in the world, those people must be evil, easily identifiable, and inhuman in certain ways. This is often true. The evils of Nazism were caused by Nazis, whose inhumanities were evident. The perils of Maoist communism were caused by coldhearted Maoists. But climate change is only slightly similar to those things. Granted, there are scheming CEOs and denialist politicians whose vicious contributions to the problem are probably much greater than those of the average citizen. But all of us participate in the process—both through tacit compliance with economic expansion and through direct engagement with it. Moreover, the human impulses that have led to climate change are usually portrayed as laudable—they are the fundamental impulses that propel our humanity, in the modern paradigm of the person. We extol the drive to hard work, a "go-getter" mentality, and taking advantage of the resources at hand. The origins of the problem reside in our virtues, not our vices.

The result of this paradox is that so long as we perceive never-ending labor as the pinnacle human virtue, the climate crisis will continue to make our heads spin. We will look for a moral hero to swoop in and save our planet, but no such character can emerge, because our fundamental moral values are the cause of our predicament.

I am not suggesting that we must replace hard work with laziness in our ethical canons, or that diligent labor will play no role in addressing the climate problem. Technology is essential for human well-being, and primitive, romantic naturalism cannot help us. Creative genius—the soaring of the human intellect—is what leads us to efficient technologies that we so desperately need, and genius is the result of hard work. Our world craves more scientists, engineers, artists, philosophers, and the practical artisans to put their ideas into action.

But all labor must eventually come to an end. Greater and greater efficiency leads to less work required. If we continue to exert ourselves beyond the point of necessity, we end up destroying our own accomplishments. We become like a sculptor who ceaselessly whittles away at the statue, constantly trying to perfect its visage, until eventually the entire project has become shreds on the ground. To avoid this outcome, the sculptor must step back at some point and say, "It is good, very good"—and set the chisel down. The full goodness of the artwork cannot exist without a decision to stop—to do nothing.

Today, human beings have not yet reached the point where we must finally lay down our chisels. We are still honing our living space on earth. Also, unlike a statue, earth is a dynamic, living artwork, of which we ourselves are a part. So there will never come a point when all productive human activity will cease. Nevertheless, if we are making real progress, we must eventually recognize the achievement of a goal, embracing who we are and what our planet is. Unlike other virtues such as honesty and kindness, diligence is one that must at times be put aside, and we struggle to understand this. There must come a point when the word *useful* takes on a different meaning, referring not to labor for acquisition of material resources, or the utilitarian remolding of the planet, but something more aesthetic, or even playful. Such an idea strikes most of us as preposterous. Millions of years of evolution and hundreds of years of industrial expansion have trained our minds to maximize output, to value the sculpting of our material resources. The specter of inoperativity looms before us, and we do not know how to comprehend it.

Enter Rituals

Fortunately, human beings have developed certain ethical tools for learning how to embrace inoperativity. They are found in religious traditions. For hundreds and perhaps even thousands of years prior to the advent of capitalism, humans in the context of religion have practiced the intentional, honest, and forthright (non)act of doing nothing. Rituals such as Sabbath, *shmita*, meditations, vigils, and fiestas have in different ways summoned human beings to cease their work and frolic in the realm of the superfluous. It is true that all these rituals have additional utilitarian purposes, such as education, mental cultivation, community development, and—in some religious mindsets—the placation of a deity. Nevertheless, at their core is an element of cessation and nonproductivity. Etymologically, the Hebrew noun meaning "Sabbath" or "Shabbat" correlates to the simple verb meaning "to stop." If we wish to learn the value of stopping, we need look no further than ancient rituals such as these.

The problem is that not everyone who engages in rituals of inoperativity does so with a consciousness of truly doing nothing. Religious persons may easily shuffle through them in a mindless, production-oriented manner. They may become yet one more objective on a working person's checklist. For this reason, if we wish truly to grasp the inoperativity at the center of rituals' being, we must carefully examine and parse them, looking at them through a sharply focused ethical lens. We must engage them as vantage points for learning how to live.

Currently, this is not a task most academic disciplines are accustomed to doing. Ritual studies are commonly the domain of anthropology, sociology, and history. Ethics, meanwhile, tends to perceive rituals as impediments to moral thought. In English, when we describe something as being done in a ritual manner, the word tends to become synonymous with "perfunctory." We thus tend to assume that no ethical awareness arises from it (as in, "ritual anti-racist training"). In Protestant Christianity, particularly, rituals may appear as the embodiments of legalism and the enemies of true moral development. Protestantism's focus on productive work casts a judgmental glare on the aesthetic, stylistic excess of ritual behavior. Even among religious observers who explicitly appreciate rituals, there may be a tendency to separate ethical reflection from direct engagement with them.

This separation is unfortunate, because rituals are the grounding points for ethical systems. David Graeber and David Wengrow, echoing theorists like Emile Durkheim, observe that basic ethical ideas such as the notion of private property and human rights have their origins in rituals.[13] The connection between rituals and ethics may be invisible to those who have become jaded to them, but it immediately appears whenever the ritual system is disrupted or altered. For example, the custom for American athletes to stand during the national anthem before televised games seemed insignificant for many years, until a few athletes decided to kneel in protest for how the nation has treated black citizens. The simple act of kneeling exposed the ethical turmoil at the heart of American patriotism and the

---

[13] This does not mean that human rights or the idea of private property are invented fiat by rituals, only that rituals serve to reinforce and ground them. As Graeber and Wengrow put it, "If private property has an 'origin,' it is as old as the idea of the sacred, which is likely as old as humanity itself." See David Graeber and David Wengrow, *The Dawn of Everything: A New History of Humanity* (New York: Farrar, Straus and Giroux, 2021), 163.

complexity of living as a marginalized person in a country one is expected to celebrate.

In a similar way, the act of ritually doing nothing reveals an ethical paradigm. This is why the command to ancient Israel to keep the Sabbath is found juxtaposed with ethical maxims such as "honor your father and mother" and "do not steal." This placement of "remember the Sabbath day to keep it holy" is not a category mistake. Sabbath keeping is an ethical way of being just as much as honesty or respect for life. If ritualized inoperativity is carried out with intentionality and conscious awareness, it can make a massive impact on how we think about ourselves and our world.

What This Book Offers

The following pages unveil an "ethics of inoperativity" for a modern society, particularly one that is obsessed with working and is beginning to suffer the consequences. Here I should provide a brief definition of the technical term *inoperativity* and the playful colloquialism I use for it, *doing nothing*, both of which appear frequently in this book (I provide a more expanded definition in the first chapter). These terms both refer to actions or states of being that have no purpose outside of themselves. In other words, they are not means to an end. The weekly Sabbath is perhaps the best example of a ritual of inoperativity, but lesser-known rituals such as *shmita* (the sabbatical year), vigils, and fiestas (a category of Latinx popular religion analyzed by Roberto Goizueta) add different dimensions to the practice of ritual inoperativity that deserve consideration as well.

To develop an ethics of inoperative rituals, this book is divided into two parts. The first section consists of three chapters that investigate the theory behind these rituals. The second section provides three chapters that apply the theory of ethical inoperativity to the problems of modern work and climate change set forth above.

In the first section, Chapter 1 explores the question of what rituals of inoperativity involve at a philosophical level. To explore this question I engage three modern philosophers whose work addresses inoperativity: Jean-Yves Lacoste, Josef Pieper, and Giorgio Agamben. Lacoste argues that basic acts of worship like prayers and vigils place human beings in a state where they automatically "do nothing"—they are rendered inoperative before the Absolute. Pieper argues that this status of doing nothing or "leisure" is not only important for religious reasons, but it establishes the only way in which humans can truly perceive the world. Agamben, probing the same idea, differentiates between two types of inoperativity. A sovereign form of inoperativity maintains the apparatus of power, while another "messianic" inoperativity disables the categories that preserve hegemonic power. Combined, these perspectives demonstrate that inoperativity is a central part of human life that can have widely varying ethical implications. This will be crucial to showing the ethical impact of inoperative rituals on practical life.

Chapter 2 investigates the theological ideas embedded within inoperative rituals, particularly Sabbath. Two thinkers, Christian theologian Jürgen Moltmann and Jewish theologian Abraham Joshua Heschel, show that within biblical theology God's own being can be understood as inoperative, setting a pattern and precedent for human identity.

Having established that inoperativity is central to human identity, we then turn to a key question: How can pointless actions be the subject of ethics? In Chapter 3 we explore a paradox that emerges from this question: Inoperative rituals are intrinsically pointless, yet they must have a point. A comparison of two approaches to inoperative rituals shows how this paradox fits together. The selected examples are early-twentieth-century chief rabbi of British Mandate Palestine Rav Kook's work on *shmita* and contemporary Catholic theologian Roberto Goizueta's approach to popular rituals in Latinx religion. Kook's advocacy for the *heter mekhira* (the partial suspension of the sabbatical year) demonstrates the idea that inoperative rituals must be able to suspend themselves to produce the context for freedom and greater inoperativity. In other words, they must be oriented toward an end or goal. Goizueta makes what initially appears to be the opposite argument. Focusing on Latinx rituals such as the fiesta, Goizueta claims that inoperative rituals must not be framed as a form of *poiesis,* or productive action, but must remain *praxis*—a form of life in themselves. Despite the apparent contrast between these two practical angles, this chapter argues that they expose two sides of liberating ritual inoperativity. To create life, it must be truly inoperative.

In the second section, Chapters 4 and 5 show how the ideas explored in the first three chapters impact ethical paradigms in two key areas. The first example, analyzed in Chapter 4, is the domain of labor. This chapter shows how the paradigm behind inoperative rituals such as Sabbath and fiesta calls us to think differently about the ethics of work within a capitalist economy. In Chapter 5 we explore how inoperative ethics summon us to reimagine approaches to the problem of climate change. Theorists usually tackle the climate problem as a technical governmental or scientific problem rather than as a struggle for human identity. This chapter presents evidence that the climate problem requires us to fundamentally restructure our view of our role within the world, placing value on living itself (sabbatical living) rather than production of material resources. We can only do this by reversing the modern tendency to see life as a means to work.

The goal in this book is to show what inoperative rituals teach us about the ethics of our everyday lifestyles, our politics, our ecology, and especially our work. Naturally, this study will fascinate members of religions that utilize these rituals, but it might also interest readers who follow no particular religion but are keen to learn what ancient rituals have to say to modern problems. If, as suggested above, a realm of inoperativity looms before all of us, we need to learn how to live with it.

I

The Philosophy of Doing Nothing

Prayer and ethics are simply the inside
and outside of the same thing.
—John A. T. Robinson, *Honest to God*

What Do I Mean by Rituals of Doing Nothing or Inoperativity, and What Do They Have to Do with Ethics?

It makes sense to establish a few preliminary definitions. First, *inoperativity* or *doing nothing.* This is admittedly a slippery and paradoxical concept, which it is part of this book's purpose to explain. As the reader likely suspects, *inoperativity* does not refer to a total vacuum of activity, as one finds in a person who is unconscious or in a deep sleep. An unconscious person is not "doing nothing," because such a person is not "doing" period. Rather than a dull cessation of activity, inoperativity refers to intentional actions or states of being that have no purposive quality outside of themselves. In other words, they are actions for which the question "why" in a teleological sense would not seem to be applicable, or would appear odd. For example, if I asked you, "Why do people want to enjoy beautiful things?" you would probably respond, "Because people want to enjoy beautiful things." You could give chemical or neurobiological explanations for enjoyment of beauty (experience of beauty produces dopamine), but these explanations are merely descriptive of the process itself, not answers for why a person chooses to rejoice in beauty. Enjoyment of aesthetics—at least in part—is an inoperative action.[1] You do not do it to accomplish something else.

Nevertheless, the paradoxical element of inoperative behaviors is that many of them *do* accomplish results that are tangible and "productive," and sometimes we are motivated to engage in them because of their positive results. For example, enjoyment of a beautiful song or painting may elevate my mood and cause me to treat people kindly. That does not mean that the purpose of the song or painting is exclusively mood elevation. Rather, it may be that *because* the artwork has no value outside of itself, I feel good as a result of perceiving it. This paradox will appear frequently in what follows. Sometimes inoperativity will appear to be motivated by a goal, but upon closer inspection it will be clear that the goal can only be achieved if the inoperativity exists for intrinsic value. Far from being a contradiction, this paradox is at the core of what inoperative rituals mean for ethics.

Speaking of *ethics*, I should define this term as well. In this investigation ethics does not refer primarily to rules or precepts about human behavior (though these certainly follow) but to a set of beliefs about what goodness is, both for humans and other entities within the world. To conduct an "ethical investigation" of things like rituals is to explore how goodness appears within those rituals and how that goodness relates to other areas of life.

What about *rituals*? This is the most slippery term I will use, given that anthropologists and theologians have never landed on a universal definition for it. Theorists are divided on whether rituals may be either formal or informal, individual or communitarian, structured or extemporaneous.[2] For the purposes

---

[1] I should observe that most human activities have inoperativity "mixed" in with other purposive elements.

[2] For an overview of the different meanings of *ritual,* see Donald E. Brown, *Human Universals* (Philadelphia: Temple University Press, 1991), 139.

of this book, my working definition will be rather broad, and perhaps most similar to the definition offered by Catherine Bell.[3] By *rituals* I refer to activities or intentional behaviors that the practitioners believe are oriented to ultimate goodness, often framed as God. For the purposes of this book, it does not matter whether these rituals occur only once in a person's life or happen regularly. What matters is that the rituals have a transcendent dimension, pointing to or relating the practitioner to something inherently good that lies beyond the immediate application of the ritual.

The conjunction of my definitions of ethics and rituals demonstrates why it makes sense to speak of an ethics of rituals. If the domain of ethics is a reflection of our belief in what is most important or ultimately good, and rituals point humans toward the good, rituals and ethics must be closely related. Also, this means that rituals and theology are tied together. The Christian church has long maintained a principle known as *lex orandi, lex credendi*—the law of prayer is the law of belief. This principle teaches that faith arises from prayer and other types of rituals, which are the real spaces where we encounter God. It also suggests that ideas about goodness come from direct encounters, and such encounters do not primarily take place in abstract theorizing but in the world of liturgy. The implication is that if we want to fully explain an ethical idea, we must explain the ritual or practice from which it arises.

The first step in understanding inoperative rituals is to take a careful look at what they are—or what happens when we do them. In this chapter we explore how inoperative rituals have

---

[3] According to Bell, a ritual is "a way of acting that is designed and orchestrated to distinguish and privilege what is being done in comparison to other, usually more quotidian, activities." See Catherine Bell, *Ritual Theory, Ritual Practice* (New York: Oxford University Press, 1992), 74. My definition, in which "ultimate goodness" plays a role, is more specific than Bell's, but that is primarily because Bell writes from a purely descriptive, anthropological standpoint.

been understood by modern philosophers who have (perhaps surprisingly) expended immense energy in thinking about them. The concept of inoperativity became a prominent theme in modern philosophy in the twentieth and twenty-first centuries, leading to fascinating reflections on what doing nothing may mean for ethics. A handful of philosophers, specifically Jean-Yves Lacoste, Josef Pieper, and Giorgio Agamben, have tackled the subject from a religious angle and provided incredible insights. Before diving into their arguments, it may be helpful first to survey a bit of background on why *inoperativity* has become a major buzzword in some sectors of the philosophical world.

Philosophers and Inoperativity—Strange Bedfellows?

Stereotypically, philosophers and other theorists focus on active events—things that we deliberately do. For example, epistemological philosophers study how human beings "do" the act of knowing. Political philosophers focus on active phenomena like wars, revolutions, coups, and acts of legislation. However, in the twentieth century, many philosophers became interested in a curious phenomenon variously called inoperativity or nonwork (what I have playfully called doing nothing) and the role it plays in social and political phenomena. Some of these philosophers pointed out that human beings deliberately do nothing all the time, and the ways in which this happens communicate much about who we are.

One example of a type of inoperativity that is different from (though related to) the type of ritual inoperativity we explore in this book is the workers' strike analyzed by philosopher Walter Benjamin in the 1920s.[4] If we look closely at unionized workers

---

[4] See Walter Benjamin, "Critique of Violence," in *Walter Benjamin: Selected Writings, Volume 1, 1913–1926,* ed. Marcus Bullock and Michael W. Jennings (Cambridge, MA: Belknap Press, 1996), 236–52.

who go on strike, we find that they do a fascinating, almost paradoxical thing. At a basic level they simply cease working. One might say that workers who are on strike are merely existing—not affecting the world. However, as Benjamin points out, their "doing nothing" is also a robust type of action—equivalent to divine violence—suspending the order of the economy and forcing changes in labor and even government. This is why a strike does not fully fit the definition of inoperativity I provided above. To the extent that striking workers attempt to change their employment circumstances through not working, their "doing nothing" is ultimately a means to an end. Still, there is an element of pure inoperativity in a workers' strike. Workers who are protesting unfair working conditions or pay may indicate through doing nothing that they are not to be treated as mere objects in a mechanistic system, that they themselves are not means to an end. The striking worker may convey that "my existence is valuable for its own sake, not just for increasing shareholder value." This aspect of the workers' strike is truly inoperative in the sense I have defined above.

But that is not all. There are other ways beyond strikes and boycotts that inoperativity arises in our world. Looking deeper into the development and maintenance of human societies, twentieth-century philosophers such as Georges Bataille, Jean-Luc Nancy, and Maurice Blanchot have argued from sundry angles that what keeps civilization together is ultimately a type of doing nothing, defined as the willingness to step back from others and simply allow them to be neighbors to us.[5] Every time I choose not to harass, rob, enslave, or kill a person I pass on the street, I help keep society from crumbling. This may seem

---

[5] See, for example, Georges Bataille, "Le temps de la revolte," in *George Batailles—Essential Writings,* ed. Michael Richardson (London: SAGE Publications, 1998), 191; Jean-Luc Nancy, *The Inoperative Community,* ed. Peter Connor (Minneapolis: University of Minnesota Press, 1991); Maurice Blanchot, *The Unavowable Community,* trans. Pierre Joris (Barrytown, NY: Station Hill Press, 1988).

like a banal point, but the history of slavery, misogyny, and genocide reveals that the impulses to do these things are deeply embedded in us, and choosing to do nothing when one feels like commencing a murderous rampage or exploiting a coworker is a significant and difficult accomplishment. The history of tolerance and liberalism is in part a story of inoperativity arising in places where it did not previously exist. If you have any doubts about this, just think about what you would do if someone told you that a witch lived next door to you, and then compare your natural reaction to "do nothing" with that of a typical 1600s European or Euro-American.

Inoperativity has not always appeared socially beneficial to philosophers. Perhaps the most negative exploration of inoperativity among modern thinkers was the famously ruthless unmasking of the "leisure class" by Thorstein Veblen in 1899.[6] Veblen argued that wealthy elites use wasteful, pointless rituals—which he dubbed "conspicuous leisure" and "conspicuous consumption"—to set themselves apart from inferior classes. Naturally, this type of leisure is not pure inoperativity in the sense I have defined it here, because it fulfills a secondary purpose, which is glorifying the leisured person. According to Veblen, members of the wealthy class seek to show dominance by leisure. This makes such leisure partly utilitarian, although those who practice it often experience it as an end in itself. Furthermore, as we will find out when we return to Veblen in Chapter 4, Veblen's rituals of leisure are—in their fullest manifestation—signs of work, intended to demonstrate prowess in predatory labor.

Doing nothing is not just a philosophical phenomenon in broad social and political dimensions. The ideas mentioned above are all related to fundamental speculations about what

---

[6] See Thorstein Veblen, *The Theory of the Leisure Class* (New York: Oxford University Press, 2007).

a human being is at a basic level. Some philosophers in the twentieth century suggested vaguely that inoperativity might be at the core of the human mind. Martin Heidegger, for example, seemed to argue in places that a human mind is a "clearing" or simply an opening within events, activities, and things.[7] Heidegger's work suggests that whatever consciousness turns out to be, it might be a form of nonaction, or a phenomenon of standing still within the whirling tumult of the world.

Describing the different ways all these philosophers use inoperativity would take a volume of its own. Still, despite the technical complexity of their work, there is a basic, common theme that emerges in their writings. In different ways almost every philosopher who reflects upon inoperativity links it to a notion of transcendence. This is, of course, a vague, heavily debated word in its own right, but it points to something we can grasp with some clarity. To experience transcendence means that one can look beyond oneself in some way. A worker who chooses to forgo a paycheck by going on strike for the greater good, or a driver who refrains from shooting at another car that cuts into the lane, or a thinker who contemplates the nature of being demonstrates a capacity to perceive the importance of a larger whole—what could be called an Absolute. The capacity to do nothing thus reveals a plane of human existence that is not instinctual or preprogrammed, but oriented toward a type of value that is both beyond and within human experience. Our doing nothing demonstrates that we are not robots, and that we can genuinely love others. It discloses our reverence for something greater than ourselves, whatever that may be.

---

[7] This idea emerges in several places in Heidegger's writings, but especially in his "Letter on Humanism," where he describes the human mind as a dwelling in an "openness." See Martin Heidegger, *Basic Writings* (New York: HarperCollins, 1993).

This "something greater" is also, of course, the focus of religious worship. Not surprisingly, therefore, we find inoperativity in liturgical rituals. What is its role there?

Lacoste: Rituals Are Always Inoperative

While thinkers like Benjamin, Nancy, and Heidegger explore inoperativity by analyzing social interactions or abstract being, Jean-Yves Lacoste takes a different approach. In his major work, *Experience and the Absolute,* Lacoste describes how inoperativity plays a central role in liturgical experience.[8] Although traditional liturgical activities such as praying or going to church only encompass a minor fraction of human life—perhaps taking up merely a few hours a week for even the most religious people—the significance of liturgy as reflective of human identity cannot be ignored. Liturgies arise from human beings' greatest struggles to apprehend the "beyond" in their experience of reality. Because these struggles are never resolved, liturgy appears fruitless in certain respects. However profound their rituals may be, human beings never grasp the Absolute through liturgy. Perhaps the best analogy for this experience is one that Jean-Louis Chretien also employs to describe prayer: Jacob's wrestling with the angel in the book of Genesis.[9] Jacob does not win the wrestling match (he gets his hip dislocated—a fairly damning occurrence in any martial contest), and thus is not able to possess or manipulate the divine. Like Jacob, who must simply sit and cling to a reality outside his control, a worshipper can only dwell passively in the presence of the Absolute.

---

[8] Jean-Yves Lacoste, *Experience and the Absolute: Disputed Questions on the Humanity of Man,* trans. Mark Raftery-Skehan (New York: Fordham University Press, 2004).

[9] Jean-Louis Chretien, *The Unforgettable and the Unhoped For,* trans. Jeffery Bloechl (New York: Fordham University Press, 2002), 122.

What happens in this act of liturgical passivity? Lacoste uses the night vigil as an example. The ritual of a night vigil is an ancient practice that is part of some pagan religions as well as Eastern Orthodox and Catholic Christianity. For the Christians who practice it, the vigil consists of staying up all night (usually from 9:00 pm to 6:00 am), praying, reciting psalms, receiving the sacraments, and often confession. These may seem like regular, functional things from a religious perspective. Nevertheless, Lacoste observes that there is a key element of uselessness in the night vigil. Night is usually reserved for sleep, which is technically a form of productivity (because the worker needs sleep in order to continue working well). But, as Lacoste argues, the night vigil "is neither a time of salaried work (*negotium*) nor a time appropriate for leisure (*otium*), for which 'free' days would be better suited than sleep-deprived nights."[10] If you want to learn the psalms for educational purposes, studying them during the day would be better than in the middle of the night. If you want to observe the aesthetic beauty of the Eucharist, it would be far easier to visit a Sunday morning service. Simply put, a night vigil is pointless. By doing it the worshipper acts in a strictly unnecessary way.

Lacoste goes further, arguing that even the most basic form of liturgy—prayer—is a form of inoperativity. "We have better things to 'do' than pray," he says, "and when we pray we actually 'do' nothing."[11] This is not the cynical accusation of a religious skeptic. Every religious tradition that speaks of a deity or higher power usually claims that this deity does not "need" prayers for any utilitarian purpose. For many religious people, this recognition leads to a quizzical feeling, if not a spiritual crisis. Most Christians who received a vigorous religious education can recall the time they first heard Matthew 6:8—"Your Father knows what you need before you ask him"—and

---

[10] Lacoste, *Experience and the Absolute*, 80.
[11] Lacoste, 73.

wondered, "Why then do we pray for stuff?" Ministers have offered lengthy and pious theological answers to this question, most of which leave serious worshippers scratching their heads. Prayer is a form of communication to the divine, but what is the point of communicating something to someone that that person already knows—especially if that person knows it better than the person communicating it? Using an analogy from the popular neologism *manspaining* (a phenomenon in which men condescendingly try to teach women about things the women are often fully informed about), a friend of mine humorously calls prayer "humansplaining." (I look forward to seeing this term in future church bulletins.) The futility of prayer seems obvious and unavoidable.

But such futility is nothing embarrassing, according to Lacoste. In fact, he says, the uselessness of prayer is the essence of its importance and what makes it so valuable for a modern, *homo faber*–oriented society. The act of doing nothing inherent in religious rituals allows worshippers to stand before God— before something outside of and beyond themselves. If night vigils accomplished something for human self-improvement, or if prayer functioned like a cosmic vending machine, rituals would turn worshippers toward themselves and their own interests. If human beings want to genuinely experience the Absolute in their rituals, they must enter a state in which whatever they are doing has no practical function. God can only be experienced from the standpoint of doing nothing.

To grasp the implications of Lacoste's argument, consider an analogy. Imagine that I am having a conversation with a friend. Ostensibly, both my friend and I are trying to get to know each other. We want to improve our friendship and develop a closer bond. Presumably, then, I want to encounter my friend genuinely—to experience him as he is. However, imagine further that I have several other goals in mind as we converse. I want to impress my friend. I want him to think I am knowledgeable and quick-witted. Hence, during our dialogue I constantly think about what I am going to say next. After I say something and he starts talking, I only listen to the parts of what he says that I think I can cleverly respond to. I reconstruct ideas he introduces so that they provide a springboard for me to utter my next debonair phrase or witty aphorism. Each time he talks I may look him in the eye, nod, and tell him his ideas are brilliant, but underneath the surface I am only listening for the purpose of doing something.

In this unfortunately common scenario, are my friend and I actually encountering each other? He may be encountering me, but I am certainly not encountering him. In fact, if my narcissistic desire to accomplish something through the conversation becomes obsessive, it would be fair to say that I am not even present in the dialogue. Our conversation would become my own monologue, and a nearly impenetrable barrier would be set up between us. The only way for me to see my friend as he is, is for me to set aside any utilitarian intentions I may have for him. A real encounter can only occur if I am willing to "do nothing" and passively allow the wholeness of who my friend is to impact me. Paradoxically, this is an integral part of what psychologists often call "active listening"—only the active part is predicated on a type of nonaction, an opening of the self toward the other person.

Prayer and other rituals that involve an encounter with the Absolute are founded on this passive openness. Why, then, do we speak specific words when we pray or keep a night vigil? In Lacoste's framework the active speech of prayer is entirely reactive. It is our way of limiting our self in the encounter. This may occur in wildly different types of prayers. For example, Augustine's famous prayer to God to "grant what you command, and command what you will" is perhaps the quintessential form of self-limitation before the Absolute.[12] But reactive

---

[12] See Augustine, *Confessions,* trans. Henry Chadwick (Oxford: Oxford University Press, 1992), X, xxix; 202.

self-limitation also emerges in prayers that may not appear to be submissive or self-limiting. For example, the raging anti-theistic bellows of Job, who chides God for being an unfair persecutor, are also evidence of a direct encounter with the Absolute. In Job's case the encounter happens as Job's suffering remains meaningless and unclarified. Job's friends try to argue that the pain inflicted on him must be just and serve a useful purpose. Their words seem to extol God's justice and demonstrate piety. Job responds by denying these claims and shaking his fist at God—and his fiery prayers reveal a God for whom suffering can never be justified. At the end of the clashing arguments and violent prayers, God responds to Job and his friends by telling them, "My anger blazes against you. . . . You have not spoken rightly concerning me, as has my servant Job" (Job 42:7). Job's prayer enables him to encounter the "real" divine, because in his speech he simply acknowledges the injustice of his situation and his anger at it. His prayer—unlike the speeches of his friends—does nothing, and that is its value.

What then do human beings do when they do nothing in worship? Lacoste's answer is simple: They stand before the Absolute, experiencing a phenomenon of overflowing grace. Does the worshipper "get anything" out of worship? Possibly yes. Lacoste does not deny the practical psychological benefits of liturgy. But these are not the essence of what happens in worship. If what the worshipper truly desires is an encounter with God, the rituals involved will always look pointless and ineffective to an outside observer. As Lacoste puts it: "Liturgy will perhaps be able to offer us the bread necessary to life. But it first offers us the wine of the kingdom."[13]

Following Lacoste, we are left with an interesting image: a worshipper standing pointlessly before the divine. A modern secular reader might object to this liturgical approach. Such a reader could argue that this is a parochial vision of inoperativity

---

[13] Lacoste, *Experience and the Absolute*, 82.

that has no relevance to nonreligious persons who do not bother with prayers or night vigils. Perhaps we might ask why standing before the divine and doing nothing should be significant for our broader understanding of the world. Is there more to inoperativity than staying up all night and praying?

Pieper: Inoperative Rituals Are Essential

I mentioned above that liturgical activity may not be a time-consuming element in many people's lives. In the modern secular world religious rituals may appear to be fading into a twilight of relevance. Nevertheless, philosopher Josef Pieper has argued that an integral element of religious rituals—which he calls "leisure"—is an innate aspect of human nature that we are in danger of losing.

Pieper is widely known for writing a fascinating study on leisure and culture entitled *Leisure: The Basis of Culture*—a book that has been somewhat misunderstood (especially in highbrow elite circles). The book is sometimes cited as an apologetic for the "leisured" classes—endowed chair academics with endless sabbaticals, wealthy arts patrons who own million-dollar businesses but rarely show up at the office, or hypergamous nonworking spouses with nannies to take care of the children.[14] My suspicion is that Pieper's work is cited by many people who have not bothered to actually read his book. Pieper does endorse leisure, but what he means by it is something far more important than having time to sip a martini at a jazz bar. Leisure, he says, is at the foundation of how we understand our world.

Pieper's argument begins by making a distinction between two types of knowing. The first type is of relatively recent vintage, and Pieper cites the philosopher Immanuel Kant as its

---

[14] See Josef Pieper, *Leisure: The Basis of Culture,* trans. Alexander Dru (New York: Pantheon Books, 1952).

foremost representative. According to Pieper, Kant describes the mind's act of knowing as an active process, in which the mind exercises "the power of discursive, logical thought, of searching and of examination, of abstraction, of definition and drawing conclusions."[15] Pieper calls it *ratio*—the root word of *reason.* Someone who *reasons* about the world takes hold of it, controls it, and makes it fit the categories of the mind.

The second type of knowing Pieper calls *intellectus.* This type of knowing is not active but receptive; it opens up the mind to the impact of the world and whatever is beyond the world. *Intellectus* is the process by which ideas, structures, and forms of meaning leave their mark on the mind. A person engaged in *intellectus* is really doing nothing, in the sense that such a person is passively being enveloped by the whole of whatever is being known.

These two types of knowing are not necessarily separate or competing. Ideally, according to Pieper, they work together. For example, consider a scholar of music who has studied the works of Bach. Such a scholar understands the theory behind Bach's compositions and perhaps has memorized the scores of countless pieces. The scholar grasps why Bach placed notes in certain places and why certain instruments are fitted for particular works. Pieper would call this scholar's knowledge *ratio.* However, knowledge of musical notation and theory is far from the only thing such a scholar does. Whenever the scholar performs or listens to a Bach composition, the scholar is affected by the music. The scholar perceives the wholeness and beauty of what Bach created and understands its meaning for human culture. This epistemic phenomenon is *intellectus.* When the scholar listens to the *St. Matthew Passion,* the scholar actively comprehends the technical brilliance of the music (*ratio*) and simultaneously also perceives the reality of its beauty (*intellectus*).

---

[15] Pieper, 11.

Although *ratio* and *intellectus* flow together smoothly, Pieper argues that it is possible to separate them. A scientist could spend years studying surveys and experimental data on the behavior of children but never sit down and listen to a child to "know" what that child is like. An ornithologist seeking tenure at a biology department might make innumerable trips into the wilderness to document the flight patterns of eagles but never stop to appreciate the glory of a soaring eagle. Of course, such complete failures of *intellectus* are rare. More likely, the psychologist or biologist would find that *intellectus* does not disappear entirely but slips into the background, gradually fading into a minimal role as the pressures of *ratio* increase.

Pieper argues that this gradual recession of *intellectus* is precisely what has happened at a general level in the modern world. Following Kant and the other philosophers of the Enlightenment and the Industrial Age, we seek not to experience the world, but to grasp it. Everything requires a "use" for us. Science provides us with utilitarian justification for the most commonplace aesthetic phenomena. We cite research on the nutritional value of eating family dinners and the serotonin boost that arises from giving hugs. We employ meditation to lower our blood pressure. Even sex becomes a technical tool for burning calories and increasing immune function. Of course, *intellectus* always dangles at the fringes of our mental operations. But we look awkwardly at it—with a mixture of embarrassment and fascination. We find ourselves pushed by a strong moral imperative to do more than simply experience the world. We must use it!

How do we restore *intellectus*? Pieper's answer is simple: We need leisure. This is where his argument easily gets distorted. Leisure, for Pieper, does not correspond to recreation, entertainment, or luxurious living. In fact, the distraction associated with pleasurable amusements can be just as toxic toward *intellectus* as overwork. Pieper points out that what monks have called *acedia*—a state of languid disinterest—is also a failure truly to perceive the world and often results in a desperate search for stimulating environments that suppress *intellectus*. Both the professor who works ninety-hour weeks to achieve maximal publication potential and receive tenure *and* the student who plays video games while smoking marijuana to forget about coursework are failing to perceive the world, albeit in starkly different ways. (This may be the common thread behind the dual elements of the "work hard, play hard" mantra.) Leisure is thus different from "having a good time," although it may indeed be rewarding and pleasurable. Leisure's essence is celebration—the practice of genuinely appreciating created reality. According to Pieper, leisure is "not the same as non-activity, nor is it identical with tranquility; it is not even the same as inward tranquility. Rather, it is like the tranquil silence of lovers, which draws its strength from concord."[16] A leisurely person intentionally stands in awe of beauty, truth, and good- ness—doing nothing, but only nothing from the perspective of *ratio*. In an ultimate perspective, leisure is the most momentous undertaking human beings can attain. Leisure is the essence of what it is to truly know the world.

Modern society must therefore aim at a leisurely existence in order to fulfill our humanity. But if entertainment does not necessarily produce leisure, and neither does diligent labor, what does? Here Pieper's argument turns toward rituals. Pieper argues that "if celebration is the core of leisure, then leisure can only be made possible and justifiable on the same basis as the celebration of a feast. *That basis is divine worship.*"[17] Pieper means that all true leisure emerges from the appreciation of the goodness of reality, and the only word for this experience is what religious people have called *worship*. A pure, non- manipulative feast is an event in which humans affirm, honor, or revere something for its inherent goodness. In such an event

---

[16] Pieper, 29.
[17] Pieper, 44.

an aspect of world impresses itself on the mind—*intellectus* occurs. Even if celebrants do not consciously think of themselves as engaging in a serious epistemic function through feasting, this is what they are doing.

Do we have enough feasts in the modern world? Not according to Pieper. We have plenty of recreational consumption, but this is not feasting in the ritual sense—it is simply distraction. Pieper claims that part of the reason for our dearth of feasting is our lack of true faith. He claims that "however dim the recollection of the association may have become in men's minds, a feast 'without Gods,' and unrelated to worship, is quite simply unknown."[18] The innumerable festivals, holidays, and sundry jubilations that litter the contemporary Western calendar year are—in Pieper's analysis—imposters. They are faux celebrations in which we honor false gods, perhaps unknowingly. For example, when many Westerners observe Christmas by buying expensive gifts or decorating their houses and tables with pricey commodities, they may be worshipping not the ultimate principle of divine generosity (in Christian terms, Christ) but the slavish values of the market system. They are not practicing leisure but worshipping work.

Still, some true celebration and leisure do occur in the modern world. Vigils, Sabbaths, and fiestas (the latter two we examine in subsequent chapters) provide a central element of inoperative perception of beauty for countless worshippers. Even outside of formal religious contexts true leisure can occur—and perhaps this is where it is most common. When I walk across the campus of my university and observe a cluster of students building a snowman, I see true leisure. What are these students worshipping? Not the snow or the snowman, but the transcendent value of community, the intangible joy of producing something pointlessly beautiful in the midst of an academic system that (increasingly) seeks to instrumentalize

[18] Pieper, 45.

beauty, science, and people. Far from being fatuous, snowman building is an expression of supernatural meaning.

Perhaps Pieper would not consider snowman construction to be true leisure. For our purposes here, it is only important to note Pieper's main claim about rituals that "do nothing"; they are a fundamental aspect of our humanity at its deepest core. We cannot know the world or comprehend who we are unless we passively perceive the goodness of what is. A world in which we do nothing but reason (*ratio*) but never comprehend (*intellectus*) is epistemically impoverished, warped, deformed, and inhumane. Furthermore, real *intellectus* requires reverence, and reverence rests on rituals. Rituals are thus not a "side project" in humanity's effort to achieve progress. They are the centerpiece of what makes us more than just computers.

Let us sum up the argument thus far. Lacoste posits that what makes religious rituals unique is that they are inoperative. They involve encountering the Absolute, the totality and limit of human reality, creating a context in which nothing can be done. Pieper shows why this is important. Religious rituals of leisure enable us to perceive fully the world and its goodness. Without them, we do not fully think.

Our philosophical exploration of inoperative rituals is not complete yet, however. While pondering Pieper's understanding of leisure and how it is different from many of the common feasts that occur in the modern world, a question emerges. If there are diverse faux types of leisure available, how do we know whether we are really practicing *intellectus*? Here perhaps another philosopher can help.

Agamben: There Are Different Kinds of Inoperativity

Before delving into how Giorgio Agamben explains different kinds of inoperativity, I should provide a bit of background about Agamben's philosophical method.

At the risk of sounding pejorative, one may describe this oddball Italian philosopher as a "squirrelly" thinker.[19] His work fits broadly into the category of political philosophy, but he pilfers ideas from innumerable other disciplines—including ancient historical anthropology, literary theory, poetry, the Bible, and church history—and he moves from one discipline to another rapidly. The reason for this massive scope of Agamben's investigations is that his topic is proportionally massive: He seeks to analyze what "life" means. His strategy is not exclusively biological. He seeks to understand how we think about life in a political sense, and how those thoughts influence the way we actually live. In the context of this vast exploration, Agamben regularly stumbles upon the concept of "inoperative" life. Before we get to his discoveries in that area, however, we must first understand how Agamben thinks about the various forms of life.

Life in human societies, according to Agamben, may be categorized in two different ways (a distinction he draws from ancient Greek thought, specifically Aristotle): *zoe* and *bios*.[20] *Zoe*, the first form of life, refers to "bare" life, the life of a subsisting creature—what biology textbooks explore. It is characterized

---

[19] Thomas Carl Wall describes the structure of Agamben's book *The Coming Community* as "crazy, slightly drunk (even as the thinking in it is precise and delicate)." See Thomas Carl Wall, *Radical Passivity: Levinas, Blanchot, Agamben* (New York: SUNY Press, 1999), 121.

[20] This distinction occurs throughout Giorgio Agamben's work, but see especially his *Homo Sacer: Sovereign Power and Bare Life,* trans. Daniel Heller-Roazen (Stanford, CA: Stanford University Press, 1998); *The Open: Man and Animal,* trans. Kevin Attell (Stanford, CA: Stanford University Press, 2003); and particularly the first chapter of *The Use of Bodies,* trans. Adam Kotsko (Stanford, CA: Stanford University Press, 2016), 3–23. The *zoe/bios* categorization is also important for Michel Foucault, a thinker with whose work Agamben often engages, as well as for thinkers such as Roberto Esposito. See Michel Foucault, *The History of Sexuality: Volume One, An Introduction,* trans. Robert Hurley (New York: Random House, 1978). See also Roberto Esposito, *Bios: Biopolitics and Philosophy,* trans. Timothy Campbell (Minneapolis: University of Minnesota Press, 2008).

by an unadorned functioning, prior to complex forms of socialization. Human beings are, in many ways, discrete biological systems, with certain basic needs and drives, summarized by scientists in terms of the "Four F's": feeding, fighting, fleeing, and sexual functioning. However, human beings do not stay as such. We form another kind of life, designated with the Greek term *bios*. This is political life, life under law, corresponding to life within the *polis*, for Aristotle.[21] *Bios* arises from the making and enforcing of institutions of law, including states, local governments, churches, universities, and social clubs. Much of Western political philosophy, from Hobbes and Rousseau to Rawls and Nozick, seeks to describe how *zoe* should be transformed into *bios*—how human beings in a "state of nature" should form political institutions that establish laws and thereby ensure rights.

Ultimately, these institutions become marked by the exercise of sovereignty. For Agamben, the sovereign is the one who guarantees that a person is more than merely *zoe*—also *bios*. This creation and enforcement of a certain type of *bios* is what Agamben, following Foucault, calls "biopolitics."[22] In most Western states this happens visibly in the process of citizenship. The United States, for example, was ostensibly founded on the premise of ensuring "inalienable rights" to human beings by granting these rights to US citizens. As a citizen, I have the capacity to play a role in political action through voting, petitioning elected officials, and taking advantage of those freedoms guarded for me by the government.

Bios does not only arise through citizenship. At lower political levels, we attain *bios* through being recognized by

---

[21] Agamben's use of Aristotle on the differentiation between different forms of life is provocative, particularly because Aristotle is not often viewed as a thinker within the "social contract" tradition. On Agamben's understanding of bare life and Aristotle's categories, see James Gordon Finlayson, "'Bare Life' and Politics in Agamben's Reading of Aristotle," *The Review of Politics* 72 (2010): 97–126.

[22] See Agamben, *Homo Sacer,* 6.

one another as free, equal persons. To some extent we all play a role in creating the *bios* of others through affirmations of their identities and freedom. A simple act such as opening the door for a stranger creates a reality of coexistence—what Martin Luther King Jr. once called an "inescapable network of mutuality."

In Agamben's analysis, however, there is a dark side to biopolitics. As political structures develop, centers of power also emerge that begin to curb and suppress the level of *bios* human beings may have. Sovereigns rarely deny *bios* life to anyone in a total and permanent sense (with the exception of permanent solitary confinement and capital punishment, which remain in some societies). Most governments have constitutions that declare that all human beings may possess certain rights to "life," and thus we may assume that denying a human being complete *bios* life for no reason is generally understood to be wrong. But Agamben points out that forcible reduction of *bios* life is surprisingly common. Sovereigns exercise their power by declaring a "state of exception" in which certain humans find themselves outside of *bios,* or in the borderlands between *zoe* and *bios.*

The major way in which sovereign powers exert this type of social force is through rituals. In Agamben's philosophy rituals are not just specific events that occur in circumscribed domains of religion. Rituals are actions that establish different forms of life. Rituals can establish *bios,* but they can also deprive humans of *bios,* or even put human beings in an ambiguous "no man's land" of existence. Rituals make us what we are, and what we are not.

Agamben uses the ancient Roman example of the *homo sacer*—a human being who, according to ancient sources, "could be killed but not sacrificed" as the model of a ritually excluded person.[23] The *homo sacer* was human, undoubtedly,

---

[23] See Agamben, 3–32.

but did not fall into the category of a fully human being who would thus be eligible for ritual death. Agamben's modern example of a site where this reduction of life happens is the concentration camp, where persons live as human beings, but with their biopolitical humanity negated. Another modern example that could be added to Agamben's analysis would be the condition of many refugees, whose native governments fail to provide them with adequate protections for their rights, but who are also denied entry into other countries.[24] Such "stateless persons" become subhuman, but in a fascinating and disturbing way. We all recognize that they are human beings in their physical nature, but they lack the capacity for "life" in the sense that citizens possess it. The disturbing and odd form of life these humans embody is the product of a ritual, namely, the ritual of establishing sovereign borders. We might not think of national borders as the result of rituals, but when you observe that many borders—especially landlocked borders or mid-ocean borders—do not occur naturally, you suddenly realize that their existence is predicated on the legitimacy of ritual declarations.

What does all this have to do with our discussion of rituals that do nothing? Agamben argues that when sovereigns negate or diminish the *bios* of certain humans, they place them in a inoperative condition. For example, consider a sovereign state that refuses to accept migrants from another country, even though such migrants have been violently expelled by war or famine. Such stateless persons are rendered inoperative—made to "do nothing." One can see this inoperativity in the vivid images of refugee camps at borderlands, where impoverished families mill about waiting to see whether they will be admitted into a new country. Many similar examples of biopolitical

---

[24] On the significance of refugees as examples of this form of life, see Giorgio Agamben, *Means without Ends: Notes on Politics,* trans. Vincenzo Binetti and Cesare Casarino (Minneapolis: University of Minnesota Press, 2000), 15–16.

inoperativity could be adduced to these, including the conditions of minorities under racist voter-suppression laws, persons with disabilities, young children, victims of bullying, and, in many cases both now and throughout history, women. All of these individuals can easily be placed by sovereign powers in positions wherein they lose their ability to act as full living agents. They can only stand in reverence before an absolute power who determines their level of existence.

Heads of state are not the only entities that seek to create inoperativity through sovereignty. This phenomenon happens on smaller scales through every hierarchical level of social organization. Most of the time sovereign inoperativity exists precisely to increase the material jurisdiction of the sovereign, often through mindless production. For example, CEOs and managers seek to reduce the autonomy and agency of both their employees and consumers by controlling corporate activity and market share. For many business wizards the ideal corporation is one in which workers function directly as extensions of the upper-level managers, existing purely as instruments. The pinnacle of this ideal is Taylorism or "scientific management," in which employees' holistic engagement with the production process is reduced to a bare minimum, allowing the manager to exercise the highest possible level of control and creating conditions for peak efficiency.[25] Taylor's model employee was someone just competent enough to perform a task well, but not intelligent or mindful enough to engage with the meaning of the task or to realize when the boss was manipulating or exploiting him or her.[26] The paradox here is that the worker under Taylor's

---

[25] See Frederick W. Taylor's classic *Principles of Scientific Management* (New York: Harper and Brothers, 1911).

[26] For an assessment of how scientific management produces the ideal "inoperative" worker, see Judith A. Merkle, *Management and Ideology: The Legacy of the International Scientific Management Movement* (Berkeley and Los Angeles: University of California Press, 1980).

scientific management is "doing nothing" from the perspective of individual agency, but doing everything from the perspective of overall production.

If "inoperativity" is a state that is valued for its own sake, sovereign inoperativity occurs when we deem instrumentality itself to be that final, ultimate state, the *telos* of human existence. Agamben argues that sovereign power tends to increase this quantity of inoperativity—it gravitates toward it naturally. Agamben characterizes this phenomenon as the pursuit of "glory"—which is the state in which agents do nothing but adulate the sovereign. Playfully using theological terms, Agamben describes the quintessential form of sovereign inoperativity:

> Inasmuch as it names the ultimate ends of man and the condition that follows the Last Judgment, glory coincides with the cessation of all activity and all works. It is what remains after the machine of divine *oikonomia* has reached its completion and the hierarchy of angelic ministries has become completely inoperative. While in hell something like penal administration is still in operation, paradise not only knows no government, but also no writing, reading, no theology, and even no liturgical celebration—besides doxology, the hymn of glory. Glory occupies the place of postjudicial inoperativity; it is the eternal *amen* in which all works and all divine and human words are resolved.[27]

Agamben's point is that sovereignty ultimately aims at a condition in which everyone exists to be arbitrarily controlled. The final form of this condition is plainly cartoonish: All the universe, every conscious entity, eternally applauds the sovereign and does nothing else. When the *bios* of all these entities

---

[27] Giorgio Agamben, *The Kingdom and the Glory: For a Theological Genealogy of Economy and Government,* trans. Lorenzo Chiesa (Stanford, CA: Stanford University Press, 2011), 239.

has been amalgamated into the sovereign, a sheer pointlessness emerges. As Agamben puts it:

> The center of the governmental apparatus, the threshold at which Kingdom and Government ceaselessly communicate and ceaselessly distinguish themselves from one another is, in reality, empty; it is only the Sabbath and *katapausis*—and, nevertheless, this inoperativity is so essential for the machine that it must at all costs be adopted and maintained at its center in the form of glory.[28]

Simply stated, inoperativity is the stasis of sovereign rule—the "in itself" of power. If all things exist for God, then God's rule over all things is a self-reflective circle. The humming of the universe has no external end. The great chain of being is immobile, and it is as if a permanent caste system is embedded in the cosmos, with God at the top, preserving a steady flow of top-down power throughout the system.

Needless to say, this is a dystopian vision of "doing nothing." If all of creation—every social form, every structure—mechanically gives glory to the sovereign, the system turns into a computer that endlessly repeats meaningless operations. Glory itself begins to collapse. The glimmering spark of *bios* fades into ash. Human beings in this inoperative state can neither love nor be loved—they can only stand motionless before the incomprehensible sovereign.

Agamben's assessment of inoperativity alerts us to a frightening possibility. Human beings in their pursuit of meaning—of the Absolute—can be lured into positions whereby they surrender their humanity and become "zombified" automatons whose existence serves only the sovereign authorities of whatever system in which they dwell. There are numerous examples of this phenomenon in the realm of religion. Many of us are

---

[28] Agamben, 242.

aware of religious people—some of whom may be in stereo-typical cults—who become inoperative, "doing nothing" except existing in the service of the cult leader or the denomination's concept of the divine. This also happens politically when we surrender our agency to a charismatic figure or ideology. At the social level the sovereign ritual of inoperativity may correspond to the click of the "follow" button on a social-media star's home page. Perhaps most disturbingly, sovereign inoperativity rears its menacing head in the economic sphere, where currency value determines the meaning of the existence of everything from soap to human beings. When I, as a consumer, mindlessly purchase an item because the market has told me I need to have it in order to be more complete as a person, I may appear to actively do something, but I actually render myself inoperative through my submission to the market. I bow before an author-ity, reverently resting in the face of a monumental edifice of power. To some extent, then, I lose my relationality—my *bios.*

Agamben's sovereign inoperativity may seem as if it is achieved through coercion or vicious manipulation, but often we willingly genuflect before it. The icons we worship offer us escape from stress and suffering, and in our harried state we easily grant them permission to shut down our minds. Like the decadent characters in Aldous Huxley's *Brave New World,* who use government-authorized *soma* to blissfully pass out for days, we drug ourselves with a paradoxical cocktail of overwork, anxiety, and thrilling entertainment. This aggressively promoted mixture of stimulants and sedatives hides from us the fact that we do not know what we are doing, and may truly be doing nothing at all—except glorifying an economy, an eternally whirling treadmill of goods and services.

Clearly, Agamben's sovereign inoperativity is vastly differ-ent from the type of "doing nothing" we have explored in the first part of this chapter. For Lacoste and Pieper, inoperative rituals reveal the pinnacle of human freedom and fulfillment. For Lacoste and Pieper, the worshipper standing before the

Absolute is in a position of total agency—the beauty of the divine infuses the worshipper with full awareness of the goodness of reality and the capacity to appreciate it. Agamben's sovereign inoperativity, on the other hand, reduces humans to static entities. Alarmingly, rituals like prayer and vigils could easily fit with Agamben's sovereign framing of inoperativity.

How do we explain the relationship between these two vastly different forms of "doing nothing"? Agamben, for his part, does not offer explicit help. In some respects Agamben's philosophy functions like a conversation with Socrates, in which we discover and clarify serious problems but do not necessarily find solutions. Agamben shows us that our world is littered with inoperative rituals—and that these rituals often reduce our humanity and serve to glorify sovereign powers. He does not tell us what to do about this.

Still, at various points in his work a glimmer of positive potential emerges. Agamben sometimes speaks of something he calls an "eternal" or "messianic" inoperativity that works against the dominance of sovereign power. His comments on this type of inoperativity are always vague. He stimulates the reader with hints at its qualities without ever tangibly describing it. While outlining the way Christian theology has understood sovereign inoperativity, Agamben cites an intriguing passage from Augustine's *City of God,* where Augustine posits an "eternal inoperativity": "After this period (the end of time) God shall be inoperative on the Sabbath, when he shall make inoperative itself that very Sabbath that we shall be."[29] This suggests that there could be a type of inoperativity that does not exist for its own sake (as sovereigns do) but exists for others.

At the conclusion of *The Kingdom and the Glory* Agamben comes closest to describing this type of inoperativity when he asks a profound question: "Is it possible to think inoperativity

---

[29] Augustine, *The City of God,* XXII: 30, cited in Agamben, 242.

outside the apparatus of glory?"[30] In other words, can human beings stand silently before the Absolute without giving themselves over to the loss of their *bios*? Can they worship without turning into machines? This question is vexing and complicated, in part because manipulative sovereigns want us to think we can worship them without the loss of our agency. For this reason, Agamben's analysis of sovereignty and inoperativity suggests that worship should always be approached with caution—beneath the veneer of joy and genuine appreciation for life may lurk aggressive impulses for dominance.

Although Agamben leaves this question without a solid answer, he suggests that a truly messianic, liberative type of inoperativity may be available to us. Agamben points out that for Paul, the messianic age is not merely future but extends into the present through Jesus Christ. "This life," Agamben argues, "is marked by a special indicator of inoperativity, which in some ways anticipates the sabbatism of the Kingdom in the present: the *hos me,* the 'as not.'"[31] What Agamben means by this "as not" is a particular type of attitude that refuses to look at the Absolute as a sovereign power. In other words, a worshipper with an "as not" mentality stands before God with a combination of reverence and nonchalance. Such a worshipper sees God as the totality of goodness, the power beyond every authority, and yet treats every ritual observance of this totality with a plucky joviality.

Agamben tries to describe this mysterious existence: "To live in the Messiah means precisely to revoke and render inoperative at each instant every aspect of the life that we live, and to make the life for which we live, which Paul calls 'the life of Jesus,' appear within it."[32] To exercise messianic inoperativity means to negate the pressing certainties that surround us—the

---

[30] Agamben, 247.

[31] Agamben, 248.

[32] Agamben, 248.

demands of social media power, the quest for status, the pressures of the market. A world in which status is the utmost value tells us that if we are not recognized by others for our wealth or achievement, we have lost our *bios*. Hence, we serve the powers above us in hope of recognition. We worship the absolute authority of labor, bodily improvement, wealth acquisition, and career escalation. We stand in awe of celebrities, politicians, and successful relatives. A messianic type of inoperativity summons us to look at all these powers as fundamentally empty—to render them inoperative from within.

The process of rendering inoperative the oppressive sovereignties of our world could begin with looking at God differently. If we think of God (or any form of power or authority) as a dominant force that demands submission, we may stand before it in awe and feel a sense of transcendence. We will lose ourselves in a type of religious bliss that can make us feel important, even treasured and loved. But when we look closely at the dynamic of this relationship, we realize that such submission leads to a meaningless glorification process in which sovereignty eliminates all true relational engagement between humans and the Absolute. A deity who controls us and demands the cessation of our own activity reveals itself to be a pointless deity. Paradoxically, the more power God wields over us, the less powerful God becomes.

If we practice worship not as the adoration of absolute power, but as tranquil presence before God, we find a way of looking at the world that restores life rather than demoting it into mechanical functioning. We find a new, liberative way of doing nothing—the type of genuine thinking that Pieper calls *intellectus*. We treat power with appreciation rather than obeisance, and in doing so we find a new grip on life. Still, Agamben's philosophy shows us that this type of inoperative life is closely mirrored by its devilish opposite, and that pursuit of the Absolute can easily lead us to a vicious form of inoperativity, one which we will have to take great pains to identify in practice.

To sum up, then, we may posit that the false, non-leisurely forms of inoperativity Pieper pointed out can be recognized by how they cause us to perceive the power of the divine. The type of inoperativity of a true Sabbath, prayer, or vigil is one that leads us to see God as a force of grace—the emanating beauty of pure goodness that upholds our freedom. The other kind of inoperativity presents the deity (or deities) as an agent of suppression, either by force or (more commonly) by distraction, compelling us to unconsciously assume that greed, selfishness, violence, and the rule of currency dictate what "power" truly is. This distinction will be important for understanding how an "ethics of inoperativity" can be meaningful.

Conclusion

Philosophies of inoperativity leave us with a fascinating, thrilling, and perhaps even disturbing vision of what happens in rituals that do nothing. Lacoste argues that such rituals are far more pervasive and common than we might think. All true prayer is ultimately a form of inoperativity in which we stand before the Absolute and encounter our humanity at its limit. Pieper's argument demonstrates something even more astounding: Doing nothing is an integral part of how we know not just theological things but the whole of human experience. The culmination of human knowledge appears as leisure, and without leisure (and the worship necessary for it) we will lose the *intellectus* that is a vital part of our human experience and exercise of freedom. Agamben, meanwhile, frighteningly shows that "doing nothing" is not a simple, safe, easy thing. One can be rendered inoperative by a sovereign power that does not liberate us with the "wine of the kingdom" (Lacoste) or the truth of the world (Pieper) but with a computerized existence.

Lacoste, Pieper, and Agamben compel us to look carefully at the sundry forms of inoperativity interlaced with our world. No matter how diligent and frenetic our working habits may be, we cannot escape doing nothing. If we vainly try to avoid it by enclosing ourselves in endless rationalization, attempting to strangle our *intellectus* with demanding schedules, robust intellectual and scientific pursuits, or lavish pleasures, we find that sovereign powers have rendered us inoperative by turning us into machines for their own mechanistic glorification. To turn a phrase from theologian Karl Rahner, we are all destined to be mystics of some type.[33] The question is, who will we worship? What kind of cessation of activity will we embody? All roads lead to doing nothing, but not every nothing is the same.

This ambiguous conclusion implies that if we wish to understand truly liberative, leisurely, messianic inoperativity correctly, we need to look closely at God's identity. Some religious traditions suggest not only that humans are inoperative before God, but that God is inoperative before humans. We explore this idea in the next chapter.

---

[33] Rahner's more precise wording, in translation, is "the Christian of the future will be a mystic or he will not exist at all." See Karl Rahner, *Theological Investigations XX: Concern for the Church,* trans. Edward Quinn (New York: Crossroad, 1981), 149. The reason I have turned his wording into "we will all" is that Rahner himself did not perceive the mystical tradition as an exclusive Christian possession.

2

The Theology of Doing Nothing

"It's all for nothing anyway," says the nihilist and falls into despair. "It's really all for nothing," says the believer, rejoicing in the grace which he can have for nothing, and hoping for a new world in which all is available and may be had for nothing.

—JÜRGEN MOLTMANN, *THE THEOLOGY OF PLAY*

For most religious observers, rituals are important because of the God(s) who established them. In other words, rituals are theological. By observing the ritual, believers say something about the nature of the deity who instituted it, and they affirm this deity's authority and power. A brief glance at religious history reveals countless examples of how this theological element of rituals usually works. The ancient Greek deity Apollo was known as the god who could tell the future. He commanded veneration at a cult site at Delphi in order to carry out his desire to communicate what would happen through the voice of a priestess, the *pythia.* Worshippers who approached Delphi affirmed Apollo's status as the god of foresight—the "far shooter" (Homer). Meanwhile, another deity named Demeter showed her responsibility for facilitating agriculture by instituting a series of rituals at Eleusis. When someone drank the ceremonial kykeon beverage at Eleusis, the worshipper was explicitly naming Demeter as the god of the domain of grain production.

In these cases and many others the connection between ritual and theology is relatively basic, because the connection is transactional. A straightforward means-end rationale governs the process. Votive offerings, petitionary prayers, and myriad types of sacrifices were almost always intended to *accomplish* something through the deity into whose jurisdiction the ritual fell. Ancient Harrapan warriors who sang a hymn of praise to Indra were often seeking Indra's help in battle. Mayan worshippers who spilt their blood on an altar to Tohil were likely seeking assurance of rain and fertility. The theology behind these rituals may have nuances and esoteric aspects, but in basic form it can be explained as divine-human labor exchange. Do something good for the god, and the god will do something good for you.

This is why one of the most ancient extant religious practices—the ritual of Sabbath—is profoundly weird. In Jewish and Christian traditions God commands Sabbath observance, directing human beings to rest. What practical goods does God receive from this behavior? The smoke of a burnt offering, the sweet aroma of incense, the beauty of an icon, a song of praise—all these things might produce a tangible effect that an anthropomorphized God could appreciate. But why would God ask humans to do nothing?

As if that were not confounding enough, the first appearance of Sabbath in the Jewish and Christian scriptures suggests that the ritual is rooted not primarily in divine command but in imitation of divine activity—or, more accurately, non-activity. The passage states: "On the seventh day God completed the work he had been doing; he rested on the seventh day from all the work he had undertaken. God blessed the seventh day and made it holy because on it he rested from all the work he had done in creation" (Gen 2:2–4). The text gives no explanation for why God does this. Was God tired? What did God's rest involve?

If we can figure out the meaning of God's rest on the Sabbath, we will have accomplished a key step in determining what rituals of inoperativity could mean for ethics. Sabbath is only one of these rituals. However, because Sabbath is perhaps the most illustrious and influential inoperative ritual in world religions, it makes sense to focus on its theological meaning.

Throngs of theologians throughout history have analyzed Sabbath as a ritual prescription. However, in the modern world there are not many who have explicitly reflected on what Sabbath means *theologically,* that is, what it communicates about Godself. Two thinkers who have done exactly this—Jürgen Moltmann and Abraham Joshua Heschel—serve as the touchstones for this chapter. Their significance emerges largely because they manage to distill and vivify centuries of interpretations and traditions in a way that has commanded respect across Christianity and Judaism. Their insights will be important for applying the ethical themes that emerge in later chapters in this book.

Wrestling with God's Rest: Concepts from Moltmann

In order to understand Moltmann's understanding of divine rest, we must return to the narrative of creation in Genesis. As most readers of the biblical story are well aware, Genesis 1 depicts creation happening in sequential steps, through the span of a week. First, there is light. Then, in order, come the heavens and the ocean, the earth, plants, the sun and stars, fish and birds, animals, and finally human beings. Last of all comes the Sabbath. Obviously, the story did not have to go this way. An almighty creator could make everything happen all at once. But the story is told with a gradual plot to reveal a dramatic unfolding—creation builds toward a climax.

Many modern readers might assume that this high point of the story is the creation of human beings. Are we not the ultimate purpose of creation? After all, we are made after the fish, birds, and other animals. We are given the illustrious title "image of God" (Gen 1:26). The creator gives us dominion over the other creatures and the privilege of using the flora world as sustenance (Gen 1:28–29). What could be more important than we are?

The self-flattering, anthropocentric reading of the story makes sense partly because of the artificial division of the chapters in Genesis, which concludes the creation story with the advent of humanity in chapter 1. Nevertheless, most literary scholars argue convincingly that chapters 1:1—2:4 of Genesis were originally a single unit, later being joined with 2:4 onward. The implications of this fact are quite striking: The crescendo of creation does not arrive with humans. What the ground is to plants, and plants are to animals, humans are to Sabbath. On this basis, Moltmann observes that "it is impossible to understand the world properly as creation without a proper discernment of the Sabbath."[1] The Sabbath is not something that happens *after* creation; it is a vital part of creation itself, its end goal.

According to Moltmann, placing the Sabbath at the pinnacle of God's creative activity in Genesis makes an enormous difference in how creation is understood. Furthermore, Moltmann argues that the significance of the Sabbath within the creation has not been fully recognized. Christian theologians and preachers have focused on the six days of creation and have neglected the seventh day, and thus God has been viewed "as the one who in his essential being is solely 'the creative God' as Paul Tillich says."[2] Modern readers tend to focus on the "stuff" God makes in the creation story. This is perhaps even more the case when modern readers approach Genesis through an ethical

---

[1] Jürgen Moltmann, *God in Creation: A New Theology of Creation and the Spirit of God* (Minneapolis: Fortress Press, 1993), 277.

[2] Moltmann, 276.

lens. To give one recent example, Leon Kass's seven-hundred-page ethical commentary on Genesis devotes only two pages to God's Sabbath rest.[3] In modern (mainly Christian) mindsets God is the almighty, the robust ruler who establishes authority by *doing things.* When we think of creation, we often imagine a powerful, booming voice echoing through the cosmos, forcing existence where there previously was nothing. In this framework God's rest looks uncanny and unsettling. God creates everything in order to do nothing.

Of course, lest the reader has not already figured it out, "doing nothing" is a heuristic oversimplification. As established in the previous chapter, doing nothing or inoperativity does not refer to pure cessation of activity, but to pointless activity. For the Genesis author, God clearly was doing things on Sabbath. Genesis text says that "God blessed the seventh day and made it holy" because God rested on it. Logically, then, God's rest is not simply a vacuum of activity—it includes blessing the day and making it holy. We are therefore faced with a major theological enigma. God's rest is certainly a type of doing nothing—the word for Sabbath literally derives from the Hebrew word for "stop"—but there is a paradox here that needs further clarification. We need to seriously consider what God's rest truly means.

Although the history of theology delivers a deafening silence on the subject of God's rest, there are a few exceptions to this trend, and Moltmann is one of them. His volume *God in Creation* offers a series of stirring observations about what God's rest in creation means. First, Moltmann points out that God's rest suggests that God's acts of creation are themselves very different from what we usually think of when we use the word *create.* In a world highly conditioned by the industrial and technocratic eras, we assume that creation is always for

---

[3] See Leon Kass, *The Beginning of Wisdom: Reading Genesis* (Chicago: University of Chicago Press, 2006), 52–53.

instrumental purposes. Cars, planes, and computers are things that human beings grasp and employ for human ends. The modern process of technical creation does not end with rest—it ends with further action. Metaphorically, our creations stand before us, ready to hand, tools for our economic whims.

According to Moltmann, the conclusion of the first Genesis creation narrative with Sabbath communicates a strikingly different idea of creation. By entering a Sabbath on the seventh day, God comfortably abides "*with* and *alongside* creation," not merely "*in front of* or *behind* creation."[4] Moltmann uses these spatial metaphors to convey that God's acts of creating are not *for* any purpose outside of God's own communal fellowship with creatures. Moltmann struggles for language to describe this intimate process:

> By "resting" from his creative and formative activity, he allows the beings he has created, each in its own way, to act on him. He receives the form and quality their lives take, and accepts the effects these lives have. By standing aside from his creative influence, he makes himself wholly receptive for the happiness, the suffering, and the praise of his creatures. . . . The God who rests in the face of his creation does not dominate the world on this day: he "feels" the world; he allows himself to be affected, to be touched by each of his creatures.[5]

This language of affectation and feeling connects Sabbath to Moltmann's doctrine of the Trinity, in which God exists as mutual, egalitarian fellowship of Father, Son, and Spirit. In the context of his theory of the Trinity, Moltmann observes that "fellowship does not subject but allows others to be themselves," implying, therefore, "openness to one another, sharing

---

[4] Moltmann, *God in Creation,* 279.
[5] Moltmann, 279.

with one another and respect for one another."[6] The upshot of this theological argument is that God's fellowship existence is also the way God "rules" the world—it is God's dominion over the cosmos, the foundation of God's authority. Sabbath, then, indicates that God is not a gigantic Henry Ford or Steve Jobs, who engineers reality by grasping and manipulating material items, turning them into mechanisms for serviceable ends. God does not *make* things exist; God *loves* them into existence. Creation is therefore a direct result of God's existence as love. In the language of Ilia Delio, in creation God "becomes whole" with the world.[7]

Moltmann points out another fascinating element of God's rest in Genesis—that it never seems to end. The text does not say, "God rested . . . and then started working again after the seventh day." Perhaps the original writer assumed God kept working but never bothered to confirm it. However, it could be that this odd feature of the story is intentional. If so, Moltmann offers an explanation for it: Sabbath rest is not incidental to God. God never stops Sabbath-keeping because, in Moltmann's words, "Sabbath manifests his Being."[8] What Moltmann means is that God's existence is "intrinsically relational"—God is the love shared by people resting in one another's presence.[9] The end point of creation is not a never-ending cycle of doing stuff. It is a passive appreciation of persons in community.

---

[6] Jürgen Moltmann, *History and the Triune God: Contributions to Trinitarian Theology,* trans. John Bowden (London: SCM Press, 1991), 57.

[7] See Ilia Delio, *The Emergent Christ: Exploring the Meaning of Catholic in an Evolutionary Universe* (Maryknoll, NY: Orbis Books, 2011), 34.

[8] Moltmann, *God in Creation,* 280.

[9] The idea that God's being present with human beings is inherently relational and liberative is also central to the work of Elizabeth Johnson, who defines the divine name as "I shall be there, as who I am, shall I be there for you," thus conveying that "to be means to be with and for others, actively and concretely engaged on their behalf." See Elizabeth A. Johnson, *She Who Is: The Mystery of God in Feminist Theological Discourse* (New York: Crossroad, 2002), 241.

If Sabbath is the climax of creation and the very existence of God, Sabbath must also be where history is headed—the future of everything. Using language from Franz Rosenzweig, Moltmann affirms that Sabbath is simultaneously the "feast of creation" as well as the "feast of redemption."[10] The Jewish story of creation is for Moltmann a "prophetic tradition"—its point is not to recall a mythic legacy or provide a scientific account of origins. Instead, it charts a path for the future, awakening hope for God's trajectory in history. Moltmann argues that the redemption of the world will occur as a repetition of the Genesis account:

> Heaven and earth, the visible and the invisible, will be created anew, so that they may become the cosmic temple in which God can dwell and come to rest. Then the presence of God will fill everything, and the powers of chaos and annihilation will be driven out of creation. That is the all-pervading cosmic indwelling of God, the Shekinah. Towards that indwelling God's creation Sabbath already pointed. The true creation is not behind us but ahead of us.[11]

By this account the human celebration of Sabbath is an anticipation of a new world governed by a sabbatical mentality.

If God's goal in creation, God's present existence, and God's future are all defined by Sabbath rest, this raises a key question: How is God's inoperativity on the seventh day different from the type of sovereign inoperativity we found in Agamben's work in the previous chapter? Remember that for Agamben, sovereign powers exercise their power by creating a type of "doing nothing" in which subjects gradually lose their agency. The sovereign creates an apparatus that coercively manipulates

---

[10] Franz Rosenzweig, *The Star of Redemption*, trans. Barbara E. Galli (Madison, WI: University of Wisconsin Press, 2005), 334.

[11] Jürgen Moltmann, *Ethics of Hope,* trans. Margaret Kohl (Minneapolis: Fortress Press, 2012),129.

persons into non-*bios* life—life in service of the sovereign. This inoperativity turns humans into instruments that glorify the sovereign in a treadmill-like hum of constant activity with no purpose outside of returning honor to the sovereign.

Moltmann's interpretation of the God of Sabbath depicts a situation completely antithetical to this type of inoperativity. The deity of Genesis does not rest in order to subjugate the world but to liberate it. The idea that God rests *with* the world indicates that God's inoperativity is nonhierarchical, focused on creating a fellowship between God and creatures rather than a one-way regime of glorification. The God of Sabbath is deeply enmeshed with creation yet is not a coercive force within creation.[12]

Moltmann's idea that God rests *with* creation also signals that God's rest on the Sabbath is drastically different from some other ancient images of deities whose rest does correlate with Agamben's sovereign inoperativity. As classical scholar Mary Lefkowitz observes, the Greek gods such as Zeus, Hera, and Athena who dwell on Mount Olympus "live at their ease . . . free from cares," and regularly "take time off for rest and feasting."[13] The fact that these gods rest might appear to establish a parallel between the ancient theologies of Hesiod and Homer and the theology of the Hebrew scriptures. However, there is a drastic difference in the type of inoperativity these deities enact. For Hesiod, Zeus's rest signals his superiority over and distance from human life. Lefkowitz points out that in Hesiod's *Works and Days,* the gods make humans work so that they cannot experience the type of blissful relaxation that the

---

[12] This, according to Poul Guttesen, is the hallmark of the "regime change" depicted in Moltmann's vision of the new earth and also the central focus of the Book of Revelation. See Poul F. Guttesen, *Leaning into the Future: The Kingdom of God in the Theology of Jürgen Moltmann and the Book of Revelation* (Eugene, OR: Pickwick Publications, 2009).

[13] Mary Lefkowitz, *Greek Gods, Human Lives: What We Can Learn from Myths* (New Haven, CT: Yale University Press, 2003), 25, 82–83.

Olympian deities enjoy.[14] The gods' rest is not communitarian but feudal and aristocratic. Their rest corresponds to a sovereign type of inoperativity—it exists to instrumentalize subjects beneath it. By contrast, the deity of Genesis 2 establishes a pattern of rest that becomes the model for human participation. Later in the Pentateuch (Ex 20:8–11) humans are not only invited but commanded to join in God's rest—not to lose their agency, but to reaffirm their free connection to God. Sabbath thus shows that God's position within the cosmos is not that of a master who controls, but that of an exemplar who asks not for submission, but for fellowship. Sabbath is God's way of being present within creation in a powerful yet liberating way.

This explains why, for Moltmann, God's rest is not incompatible with the idea that God's creative potential is constantly upholding and renewing the world. Moltmann finds this dynamic in Jesus's healings on the Sabbath in the New Testament. By healing on the Sabbath, Jesus replicates the divine Sabbath keeping of Genesis by giving rest to the sick. Although Christian interpreters have often depicted Jesus as offering a "higher ethic of love" that eliminated or subordinated the Sabbath command, Moltmann notes that Jewish rabbinic tradition agreed with Jesus that the "Sabbath was made for man, not man for the Sabbath."[15] According to this view Sabbath and the love ethic are not opposed but complementary. Sabbath exists to liberate human beings from material constraints that suppress life. Because both Jesus and most Jewish traditions hold this point, Moltmann argues that Jesus's Sabbath conflicts reflect an intra-Jewish interpretive situation rather than a Christian-versus-Jewish situation.

However, this does not mean that Jesus's Sabbath observance contributes nothing new to an understanding of God's rest. According to Moltmann, what Jesus proclaims through

---

[14] See Lefkowitz, 25.

[15] See Moltmann, *God in Creation,* 291.

his Sabbath behavior is not "a higher ethic" but "the imminent kingdom of God, whose unparalleled closeness he authenticates through the signs of the messianic age."[16] Moltmann cites Matthew 10:7–8, according to which Jesus introduced this messianic age with particular actions: "The blind receive their sight, and the lame walk, the deaf hear, and the dead are raised up, and the poor have the kingdom promised to them."[17] By doing these actions on the Sabbath, Jesus takes the future-pointing trajectory of the Sabbath and brings it to completion. Thus, according to Moltmann, "Jesus never 'transgressed' the Sabbath commandment, and he certainly never made it 'a matter of indifference.'"[18] What Jesus did do was keep it in accordance with the logical outcome of the Genesis creation trajectory—as an anticipation of the kingdom of God, in which everything in the world would be put right, including blind eyes and crippled spines.

For Moltmann, the sabbatical trajectory of Genesis is rooted in the idea of humans as made in the "image of God." This status marker is far from uncontested today, both by theologians and scientists. The latter point out that humans were never perfect, and the former allege that we are certainly far from perfect now. But for Moltmann, these perspectives miss the entire point of the concept. Moltmann argues that the image of God is not an abstract status marker, but a *telos* for humans—it is our "real future."[19] We are creatures oriented toward manifesting this image in progressively starker ways. This means that our journey as created beings directs us toward dwelling on earth as God does. In this reading the structural endpoint of creation in Sabbath rest acquires massive significance. If God's existence culminates in Sabbath, ours must do the same. If we

---

[16] Moltmann, 291.

[17] Cited in Moltmann, 291.

[18] Moltmann, 292.

[19] Jürgen Moltmann, *On Human Dignity: Political Theology and Ethics,* trans. M. Douglas Meeks (Philadelphia: Fortress Press, 1984), 22.

are made in the image of God, we fully and truly exist as sabbatical creatures.

Once we realize that rest is central to God's identity and thus also the image of God, the "wonky" concept of God doing nothing becomes crucial to some of the most pressing issues raised in the introduction to this book. If Sabbath points to a God who rests, human beings cannot define themselves purely as *homo faber* but must recognize their full humanity even without accomplishing productive work.

For Moltmann, this means that human beings must not only be inoperative at times, but that rest must also become part of work. This point becomes clear in Moltmann's discussion of "the right to meaningful work." In *On Human Dignity* this right is the first concrete human right he analyzes. Such privileging of labor-ethics initially appears odd, because most books on human rights begin with "the right to life" or "the right to avoid bodily harm."[20] Moltmann certainly values these rights, but his account focuses on work because—as shown above—rights are grounded in the human enactment of the image of God, which is a functional image. In order for human beings to manifest God's image, they must be given the opportunity to act meaningfully (of course, a perceptive logician would immediately recognize that this presumes the rights to life and evasion of bodily harm—but those points would go without saying).

---

[20] The epitomic example of this is the United Nations General Assembly's Universal Declaration of Human Rights, which begins with the rights to life, liberty, and the security of persons. For an overview, see William A. Edmundson, *An Introduction to Rights* (New York: Cambridge University Press, 2004), 105–7. Other examples of theoretical works that downplay the right to meaningful work include Tibor R. Machan, *Individuals and Their Rights* (LaSalle, IL: Open Court, 1989); and Loren Lomasky, *Persons, Rights, and the Moral Community* (New York: Oxford University Press, 1987). For surveys of different theoretical approaches to specific human rights, see Michael Freeman, *Human Rights* (Cambridge, MA: Polity, 2004); and Jack Donnelly, *Universal Human Rights in Theory and Practice* (Ithaca, NY: Cornell University Press, 2003).

What is meaningful work? Moltmann points out that much work is done simply for the sake of survival, to gather sustenance and construct shelter—what is sometimes called "alimentary" work. Moltmann notes that it is possible to construe such work as neither fulfilling in itself nor a particularly creative act—it simply continues biological processes. Especially in ancient times, human existence had to be "wrested" from a hostile environment, and as Moltmann puts it, "this struggle itself was not true life but only its precondition."[21] In many ancient cultures, this was the only definition of work available. Consequently, work was devalued, and those who did not have to work (such as rulers or elite classes) would intentionally avoid degrading themselves in "common labor." Work was base, but rest was divine.

Moltmann points out that the Christian and Jewish scriptures do not accept this paradigm. In Genesis, God's creative activity does not reduce God's position in the hierarchy of the cosmos or make God less virtuous. Rather, God's glorious identity is rooted in God's willingness to work for human liberation.[22] God's work is noble, and human beings should model God in their work. However, for Moltmann, God's work can only be properly understood as virtuous when linked with God's rest. This is because godly work is participation in the innate goodness of created being—goodness that is only accessible through rest. In this way rest redefines the concept of meaningful work:

> Work is thus meaningful not because it alone provides the meaning of life, but precisely because it is limited by the goal of rest and joy in existence. The Sabbath does not simply interrupt work. Rather, work is understood and defined through the Sabbath. There is more to this ordered

---

[21] Moltmann, *On Human Dignity,* 38.

[22] Per Moltmann: "Certainly, Yahweh is no subordinated worker-god. Rather, he is the slave-freeing God, as the first commandment states, 'who led you out of the house of bondage'" (Moltmann, 40).

relationship of work days and holidays than just mutual boundaries. Work day and Sabbath lie also on the same temporal level. They concern the same people. They are not divided between human beings and gods or between slave and free. Therefore, they also overflow into each other and affect each other.[23]

When Moltmann says that work and rest "overflow into each other," he suggests that the work-rest relationship is cooperative, but not in a tensile manner. In Moltmann's understanding of God's rest, work is to rest what the white is to the black on this page. The two colors exist on the same level and they work together, but it is obvious that the one (the black writing) provides the primary distinguishing element of the entire structure. God's work is important, but it is not the primary feature of God's existence—God's rest is.

Because God's creation work forms the model for human work, Sabbath also stands as the criterion for dignified human labor. It is not that human beings must have a Sabbath so that they can go back to productivity more effectively. Rather, work exists to make Sabbath more effective. Moltmann's logic leads to an important ethical conclusion: "Therefore human work cannot consist only in acting for purpose and usefulness. It must also encompass freedom for self-presentation and thus playfulness."[24] In other words, human work must be sabbatical as well as materially fruitful. This idea of work conditioned by Sabbath will prove essential for the ethics of labor I return to in Chapter 4.

The image of God resting may sound ethereal and far removed from how we live, but it should now be clear that it completely destabilizes the standard *homo faber* paradigm of human value. Nevertheless, an important theological question

---

[23] Moltmann, 41.
[24] Moltmann, 41.

remains unanswered: What is Sabbath, actually? If the creation story shows God's nature defined by Sabbath, and human beings find their purpose in the image of God, what happens in this Sabbath leisure? What does God do when God does nothing?

A Temple in Time: The Sabbath in Abraham Joshua Heschel

Defining what Sabbath is seems easy at first. Obviously, it is a time of rest. It might be tempting to immediately jump at the word *rest* in that definition, but according to one of the most important interpreters of Sabbath, it is vital to first focus on the word *time.* Sabbath is, prior to anything else, a specific type of time. If we understand the nature of that time, it will become easier to understand what God does on it.

Jewish theologian Abraham Joshua Heschel explores the type of time Sabbath constitutes in *The Sabbath: Its Meaning for Modern Man.*[25] Despite its small size, this work holds mammoth status among modern theologies of Sabbath. Part of its uniqueness stems from its creative straddling of genres. It is equal parts poem, philosophical treatise, midrashic interpretation, and theological exhortation. But what makes it worth attending to most of all is its argument that Sabbath is not simply a ritual or a practice but a different kind of existence altogether. It is, according to Heschel, a "temple in time" that God and humans inhabit together.

To understand what this means, it is first necessary to explain how Heschel views the categories of time and space. As he states at the beginning of *The Sabbath,* "In technical civilization we expend time to gain space."[26] By space, Heschel means something incredibly broad—both material elements as

---

[25] Abraham Joshua Heschel, *The Sabbath: Its Meaning for Modern Man* (New York: Farrar, Straus and Giroux, 1951).

[26] Heschel, 3.

well as the status and pleasure afforded from physical involve-ment in the world. Modern humans who go to work five days a week give up a large portion of their time, and in exchange they get space, defined variously as property, the ability to go on vacations, food, clothes, and automobiles. There is noth-ing intrinsically wrong with this exchange. It is, after all, the foundation of human survival. However, space is seductive. Unknowingly, human beings can become enamored with space and forget about the value of time. Consequently, human beings may subject time to the exclusive purpose of space mastery. In this way human beings create a deep existential discordance: "Life goes wrong when the control of space, the acquisition of things of space, becomes our sole concern."[27]

Obsession with spatial things may sound like a problem only of rich real-estate developers or commodities magnates, but Heschel's diagnosis applies more widely than we might expect. Upon close introspection we might be surprised how much of our waking hours are consumed with thoughts of spatial things. Even artists—those quintessential idealists—often gauge their success by how many people have seen their art, and therefore how much space the art occupies (in a literal sense, all persons who view or listen to a work of art produce a copy in their brain which then occupies space).

In contrast to the space-obsessed world, Heschel claims that the "Bible is more concerned with time than with space."[28] Heschel demonstrates this by referencing the Jewish yearly festivals and feast days, which commemorate spatial events (the Exodus from Egypt, for example), but do so by "hallowing" the specific times in which those events occurred.[29] The Sabbath is the pinnacle of the various biblical time celebrations, not only because it occurs weekly, but also because it celebrates creation

---

[27] Heschel, 3.
[28] Heschel, 6.
[29] Heschel, 7.

("remember the Sabbath day to keep it holy . . . for in six days the Lord made the heavens and the earth"). Thus, to the extent that the day "commemorates" something, it is existence itself, or rather "being as such" that is commemorated. "It is a day on which we are called to turn from the results of creation to the mystery of creation; from the world of creation to the creation of the world."[30]

Sabbath, then, is less like a discrete ritual and more like a fundamental feature of the world that we can choose to ignore or accept. It is pure time—a form of reality that does not exist for the purpose of spatial activity. Thus a Sabbath keeper—whether God or a human being imitating God—enters a different dimension when keeping Sabbath, experiencing time itself. Hence, as pointed out above, Sabbath is, in Heschel's words, "a temple in time."

What does it mean to experience time itself? Heschel's view of Sabbath suggests that this experience refers to stepping aside from the material world and simply appreciating it. It corresponds closely with Pieper's leisure—the act of receiving the goodness of reality. We should not understand this experience in an anti-material way. Heschel's solution to modern materialism is not the rejection of materiality in favor of an ethereal realm of pure spirit—the solution of the ancient Gnostics and some modern religionists who seek ultimate value in alternative dimensions. Rather, Heschel's alternative is a type of celebration of the totality of existence that embraces the world and all its material goodness without attempting to manipulate or change it.

Heschel's theory of Sabbath gives us an explanation of why God rests as the ultimate culmination and goal of creation. As a creator, God exists before and in spite of material reality. God creates not because God needs material things, but because God loves the world and appreciates its inherent beauty

---

[30] Heschel, 10.

and goodness. God thus gets no "benefit" from creation in any utilitarian way but still views the world with compassionate appreciation. How, then, does God experience the world in this state? If God were to never cease creative activity, that would imply that the world is never truly good. God would be the type of perpetually dissatisfied artist who never stops tinkering with projects. But because God loves the world, God cannot abandon it, like a builder who puts a house together and sells it, never to think about it again. To appreciate creation, then, God does something that enables God to be close to creation while still allowing it to be what it is: God enters time. The Sabbath is the name of this "pure time" where God dwells with the created world for no other reason than that it is "very good."

This means that, for Heschel, God's rest is not at all like a modern vacation. Heschel's view of God's Sabbath distinguishes it from other forms of "time off" humans take in the modern world. Everyone knows we must rest or sacrifice our long-term productivity. Hence, we have company retreats, summer vacations, and bean bags at Silicon Valley business headquarters. In this quotidian sense, therefore, one might say that nearly every healthy American practices Sabbath in some form. Heschel notes that Philo defended the Sabbath against its Roman detractors (who used it to inveigh against supposed Jewish indolence) by appealing to this utilitarian aspect of Sabbath. Philo argued that "a breathing spell enables not merely ordinary people, but athletes also, to collect their strength with a stronger force behind them to undertake promptly and patiently each of the tasks set before them."[31] Under this paradigm, in which the Sabbath is simply a weekly "breather," Heschel's lofty interpretation of the Sabbath seems unduly flamboyant.

Heschel responds to Philo's trivializing apologetic for the Sabbath by pointing out that for Philo, "Sabbath is represented

---

[31] Philo, *De Specialibus Legibus,* II: 60, quoted in Heschel, 14.

not in the spirit of the Bible but in the spirit of Aristotle."[32] Leisure taken for the sole purpose of enhancing labor is not wrong or unnecessary, but it is not sabbatical at all in Heschel's sense. The Bible and Jewish traditions, Heschel argues, depict the Sabbath not as a means to an end (further work), but as an end in itself. "Man is not a beast of burden, and the Sabbath is not for the purpose of enhancing the efficiency of his work," Heschel asserts.[33] Because the Sabbath concludes creation, Heschel argues that metaphorically and literally the Sabbath is creation's "end."[34] In Heschel's succinct words, "The Sabbath is not for the sake of the weekdays; the weekdays are for the sake of Sabbath."[35] The Sabbath's existence is categorically independent. In Heschel's summation, "The Sabbath is the presence of God in the world, open to the soul of man."[36]

To appreciate the Sabbath as a "place in time" seems, therefore, to do more than exercise a religious ritual (if a "religious ritual" is defined as a means to a religious experience of some sort, the likes of which may vary between religions and cultures).[37] Heschel's framework indicates that the Sabbath is indispensable for all human fulfillment. It is not a culturally or religiously localized practice, as if it were merely "for the Jews" or "for the Christians"; it is the condition of the possibility of full humanity for everyone. As Morton Fierman observes, in his work on the Sabbath Heschel "has introduced to us a veritable prescription for living, an itinerary for life, indeed a

---

[32] Heschel, 14. Aristotle argued that rest from labor is "not an end" but simply a means for renewing activity. See Aristotle, *Nicomachean Ethics,* X: 6.

[33] Heschel, *The Sabbath,* 14.

[34] Heschel, 14.

[35] Heschel, 14.

[36] Heschel, 60.

[37] Heschel explicitly contrasts the Sabbath with other Jewish rituals such as Yom Kippur: "Unlike the Day of Atonement, the Sabbath is not dedicated exclusively to spiritual goals. . . . Man in his entirety, all his faculties must share its blessing" (Heschel, 19).

spiritual map for humanity."[38] For Heschel, then, the biblical traditions of Sabbath hint at an ethic—a means of describing human goodness in the world. At the same time, because the Sabbath is the way God exists, Sabbath presents a theology. The question "What is the Sabbath?" becomes equivalent to the question "What is God?" We are in deeper waters than we might have first thought.

Heschel's argument that Sabbath describes the existence of God casts a sober shadow over our heady attempt to describe what God does on Sabbath. "Doing nothing" is a sensible answer, but as we have seen, this phrase is deceptively simple. The "nothing" God does on Sabbath is only "nothing" from the perspective of our modern obsession with materiality. There is clearly much more to be said about what God's rest looks like.

The problem with saying more about God's rest is that doing so involves applying language to God. In both Jewish and Christian tradition, speaking about God's essential being is inevitably hubristic, because the human mind thinks with images. To make an image of God (whether in stone or in cerebral neural structures) is idolatrous. One can freely speak about the fact that God exists and the impacts of God's activity, but to speak about *what God is* thrusts us into theological peril. Yet that seems to be what the task of describing Sabbath involves.

We might give up and say that Sabbath is a mystery—and that would not be entirely wrong. But there is a possible solution found in what theologians have called the apophatic method, or "negative theology." Simply put, the apophatic method is the act of saying what God is not, rather than what God is. It allows us to speak about God in a way that keeps human epistemic limitations constantly in view, allowing for the total freedom and transcendence of God. The apophatic speaker (and listener/reader) can thus enter the presence of God without

---

[38] Morton C. Fierman, *Leap of Action: Ideas in the Theology of Abraham Joshua Heschel* (Lanham, MD: University Press of America, 1990), 177.

grasping or confining God in the cumbersome categories of the human brain.

In a brilliant way Heschel uses the apophatic method in his description of Sabbath. Instead of writing a structural metaphysics of God's rest, he provides contrasts that point to Sabbath's transcendence by negation. The most vivid way Heschel does this is by pointing to Sabbath's opposite, which he argues is—perhaps surprisingly—covetousness. To establish the antithetical relationship between Sabbath and coveting, Heschel observes an odd feature in the language of the Decalogue: Israel is told to "keep" the Sabbath day holy. To keep, or to guard (Hebrew: *shamar*), suggests possessive desire in a way that implies a type of covetousness. But then, a few verses later, Israel is told, "you shall not covet." A tension emerges between these two commands. Why is it acceptable to jealously desire or "covet" the Sabbath when we are told *not* to covet? In true rabbinic fashion, Heschel claims that "we must seek to find a relation between the two 'commandments.'"[39] There must be an explanation for the discordance in juxtaposition.

Heschel's interpretation is that the Decalogue's injunction against coveting pertains only to things of space. The text says "you shall not covet" your neighbor's house, wife, servant, livestock, or "anything" belonging to the neighbor. Institutions of time, therefore, are excluded from the purview of the commandment. Thus, coveting the Sabbath is entirely noble and acceptable. Still, this does not explain why the text goes out of its way to use the language of coveting to describe Sabbath.

To show why this covetous language is important, Heschel adds a twist. On its own, the command against coveting in the Decalogue seems pointless. Coveting is a form of desire, and telling people not to desire is rhetorically impotent, because "we know that passion cannot be vanquished by decree."[40]

---

[39] Heschel, *The Sabbath,* 90.
[40] Heschel, 90.

If anything, telling someone not to want something creates a taboo, which can inadvertently *increase* desire by adding a mystique to the forbidden realm. Desires can only be exterminated when they are either satisfied or replaced by different and better desires.

Sabbath provides this satisfaction and replacement. Heschel points out that "the tenth injunction would, therefore, be practically futile, were it not for the 'commandment' regarding the Sabbath day to which about a third of the text of the Decalogue is devoted, and which is an epitome of all other commandments."[41] Thus the Sabbath command provides the means by which the coveting command is to be executed, because it directs covetous desire to time rather than space. Heschel writes:

> Judaism tries to foster the vision of life as a pilgrimage to the seventh day; the longing for the Sabbath all days of the week which is a form of longing for the eternal Sabbath all the days of our lives. . . . It seeks to displace the coveting of things in space for *coveting the things in time*, teaching man to covet the seventh day all days of the week. God himself coveted that day, He called it *Hemdat Yamim*, a day to be coveted. . . . It is as if the command: *Do not covet things of space*, were correlated with the unspoken word: *Do covet things of time*.[42]

Why is coveting space problematic, but coveting time is not? As I have shown, space for Heschel is the realm of control and domination. Spatial entities control us, and we seek to control them in return. In our modern era we own technology, but we know that our technology also owns us.

But covetousness of time is categorically different and antithetical to covetousness of space. To see why, consider the

---

[41] Heschel, 90.
[42] Heschel, 90–91.

moral difference between the propositions, *I need you* and *I need time with you.* The first proposition is compatible with a variety of meanings, some of them potentially dominating in Agamben's sovereign sense (imagine a boss saying, "I need you . . . to do something for me"). The second proposition suggests a much different attitude. Presumably the speaker wants to elicit a response from the listener, perhaps to do something concrete such as take a walk by the lake or go on a shared vacation. But the key feature of the sentence is that it conveys a desire for the listener's free response. The speaker does not want the recipient of the proposition to be forced to spend time. The speaker wishes for reciprocity—it is as if the speaker were saying, "I want to spend time with you, time that you also want to spend with me." Of course, it is conceivable that the speaker could, out of frustration, seek to acquire the coveted time with the listener through manipulation or outright coercion. Survivors of sexual harassment know this all too well. But intrinsically the wish itself conveys a craving for mutuality expressed through the freedom of the other.

Covetousness of time can thus be the opposite and the negation of covetousness of space.[43] Using the apophatic method, we can affirm that the existence of God is the opposite of spatial covetousness. This demonstrates the key difference between the inoperativity of Agamben's sovereign power and the messianic, sabbatical inoperativity Agamben hints at in his work. The God of Sabbath seeks inoperativity not as a mechanism of control (spatial covetousness) but as a means for liberation.

What exactly is the "time with" that God wants with us and all creation? The essence of this state or relationship falls into the category of mystery—and it might properly appear to be

---

[43] It is important to recognize that "covetousness of time" (as Heschel uses the phrase) is a type of yearning for time with creation, not time in general. As Marx could argue, the modern world has equated time with material production ("time is money") and this—in a powerful way—corrupts and demeans time, as Heschel understands it.

"doing nothing" from the spatial angle. Nevertheless, it is a "nothing" that embraces the entirety of creation in its unfolding beauty. The being of the sabbatical God is much like the experience of two lovers who spend the quiet hours of an afternoon in deep conversation, but when asked how they spent their time they reply that they were "doing nothing." Their answer reveals a more-than-casual truth. Doing nothing can be something quite important—even the very being of God.

Conclusion

Let us sum up what we have learned thus far. We found in the previous chapter that human beings become inoperative in the presence of the Absolute (Lacoste), and that this inoperativity forms a vital part of what a human being is—the end goal of human perception of the world (Pieper). Agamben showed us that the inoperativity is complex—there is a common inoperativity in which humans become servile and mechanized before the sovereign, and an inoperativity that liberates humans. In this chapter we have discovered that the God of Sabbath represents the second type. Inoperative rituals—practices that accomplish "nothing"—point to a theology that upends many traditional expectations of God's role in the cosmos. Using the enigmatic picture of God's rest in Genesis 2:1–4, Moltmann offers a vision of the existence of God as one who "lets be"—resting in the presence of creation, and inviting humans to join in this rest as recipients of the *imago Dei*.

Writing from a Jewish perspective, Abraham Joshua Heschel argues that Sabbath rest is a revelatory glimpse of God's being. The ritual of Sabbath gives us a "temple in time" in which God encounters human beings in a sacred form of existence that has no utilitarian purpose. The Sabbath is thus not "for" anything— it does not need to justify its existence. Heschel expresses the being of God as Sabbath apophatically as the antithesis of spatial covetousness—if normal human amusements and recreation consist of various types of grasping and acquisition, Sabbath consists in the opposite of these.

Although Moltmann's and Heschel's theological visions are impressive, they nevertheless leave us with a key unanswered question. If the being of God may be summed up by Sabbath rest, here defined as "being with" creation in a state of embrace, how do we ethically "apply" this state of being? So far in this book ritual inoperativity has possibly appeared esoteric and irrelevant to regular life. Simply put, if the point of Sabbath is to have no point, we are faced with a paradox when we try to conceive its practical ramifications. We explore this paradox in the next chapter.

3

The Practical Paradox
of Doing Nothing

Trample my courts no more!
To bring offerings is useless;
Incense is an abomination to me.
New moon and Sabbath, calling assemblies
Festive convocations with wickedness—
These I cannot bear.

—Isaiah 1:13

It is a warm Friday evening in Rwanda in April 1994. As crickets chirp and the last rays of sunlight glimmer over the horizon, Seventh-day Adventist workers prepare to rest. They wash their tools, placing them in the corner of their houses, ready to grab them for work on Sunday. Like most Jews, members of the Seventh-day Adventist denomination keep Sabbath from sundown to sundown, beginning on Friday. Following Jewish antecedents, within Adventist culture there is a rich tradition of "welcoming the Sabbath" by cleaning one's house and other appliances, as if an honored guest were about to arrive.

These Sabbath-keepers want to put distractions out of their mind so that they can spend the day in peaceful relaxation, worshipping and praising God. They want a momentary respite from thinking about the tools they have been using all week in vigorous manual labor.

What are these tools they are washing, tools they will pick up after Sabbath hours are over? Machetes. Why are these tools dirty? They are coated with human blood.

This is not a fictional scenario. Adventist political scientist Ronald Osborn reports that Rwanda's population at the time of the genocide was about 10 percent Seventh-day Adventist. A subset of these Adventists were Hutus—members of the ethnic group from which a faction emerged that perpetrated the killings of their Tutsi neighbors. Although many Adventists attempted to save their fellow Rwandans, Osborn spoke with a church official in Rwanda who said that "some Adventists maintained their Adventism by scrupulously resting from killing on Sabbaths."[1]

For these Sabbath-keepers, the inoperative ritual accomplished nothing for ethical practice. This phenomenon is not an isolated, rare event. The history of religious traditions is littered with examples of rituals of inoperativity such as prayers, vigils, and meditations that have no impact on ethical behavior. Countless clergy in Nazi Germany celebrated the Eucharist—an inoperative experience of pure grace—and then willingly assisted with the massacre of Jews. Can one stand before the inoperative beauty of the Absolute, experience divine fellowship, and then leave to ruthlessly murder one's neighbors? The answer might appear to be yes.

The basic problem is that inoperative rituals can be discrete events in worshipper's lives. For many practitioners, rituals represent states of being that are unconnected to life as a whole. One prays or rests, and then proceeds with "life as usual." Because the ritual is separate from daily life, it has no ethical value. The worshipper's primary ethical obligation is to perform the ritual—any other meaning of the ritual is secondary.

---

[1] Ronald Osborn, "No Sanctuary in Mugonero: Notes on Rwanda, Revival, and Reform," *Spectrum* (October 16, 2010).

Within this framework there can be no "ethics of doing nothing," because ethics involves the entirety of human life, and rituals are only a small part of life. Furthermore, resisting this paradigm is difficult, partly because inoperativity is supposed to accomplish nothing. Our definition of ritual inoperativity states that it is an end in itself, not used for some external end. How, then, do we suggest that ritual inoperativity must have ethical implications? And how do we say this without denying that ritual inoperativity is intrinsically valuable, for no reason outside of itself?

This chapter charts an answer to this question by exploring two strikingly different rituals and theologians. First, we investigate the Jewish sabbatical year, or *shmita,* and its role in the thinking of Rav Kook (Rabbi Abraham Isaac Kook). Then we compare Kook's approach to *shmita* with Catholic theologian Roberto Goizueta's understanding of fiesta and its practice in Latinx Catholic communities. The juxtaposition of these two rituals from vastly different religious environments leads us to a paradox we noted at the beginning of Chapter 1: Inoperative rituals are actions of nonaction. In other words, inoperative rituals must be goal oriented and yet pointless at the same time. Kook's work establishes the first half of this paradox; Goizueta's the second half. I argue that this paradox is the key to figuring out how rituals of inoperativity can explode the barriers of discrete rituals, becoming immensely relevant for ethical thinking.

Rav Kook:
Doing Nothing Must Do Something

Outside of certain Jewish circles Rav Kook is not a widely known figure. Nevertheless, his theological and mystical writings are vast, and his ideas influenced many important Jewish thinkers in the twentieth century. Because of his breadth of interests and his dual roles as rabbi and scholar, Kook's work covers enormous conceptual territories.[2] For the purposes of this chapter it is primarily *Rav Kook's Introduction to Shabbat Ha'aretz* (Sabbath of the land) that will occupy our attention.[3] Despite its brevity, this work contains dense reflections on the meaning of the *shmita* for the Jewish people's self-understanding. In order to understand the implications of Kook's approach to this ritual, it is necessary first to give a brief account of who Kook was, and then explain what *shmita* is and how Kook became involved in an important historic controversy about it.

A Mystical Rabbi and Political Tumult

In 1904, Kook—then an accomplished philosopher and Talmudic scholar from Poland—accepted a position as a rabbi in the newly formed Jewish community in Jaffa, Palestine. Kook was not trained as a politician. Growing up in Eastern Europe, he was enamored with books and contemplation. Nevertheless, what he faced when he moved to Palestine was a tense political situation involving rivalries not primarily between Jews and non-Jews (though such conflicts did exist) but between different approaches to Judaism.

There were two parties of Jews living in Palestine at the time, and Kook was caught squarely between them.[4] The first was known as the Old Yishuv; it consisted primarily of Orthodox Jews who had sojourned to the land of Israel for the

---

[2] For a more expansive biographical account of Kook's life, see Yehudah Mirsky, *Rav Kook: Mystic in a Time of Revolution* (New Haven, CT: Yale University Press, 2014).

[3] Abraham Isaac Kook, *Rav Kook's Introduction to Shabbat Ha'aretz,* trans. Julian Sinclair (New York: Hazon, 2014).

[4] For an account of Kook's ongoing arbitration in this situation, see Jacob B. Agus, *High Priest of Rebirth* (New York: Bloch, 1972).

purposes of piety—to pray, study Torah, and generally lead a traditional Jewish life.[5] They put little effort into the economic development of the area, relying more on charitable contributions from European Jews. The other group was the more secular Jewish pioneers known as the New Yishuv, who were intent on building up local Jewish institutions within the land. They focused on establishing a strong agricultural presence in the area.[6] The New Yishuv disdained their counterparts as hyper-religious loafers, while the Old Yishuv branded their opponents as shameless, ritually lax yuppies. The New Yishuv tended to discard traditional practices, while the Old Yishuv believed such practices were the core reason for being Jewish. It was a tense situation.

Kook valued aspects of both sides. He appreciated the New Yishuv's enthusiasm for economic development and commitment to the long-term success of the Jewish homeland. At the same time, he recognized the importance of maintaining the traditions that would sustain Jewish identity. Kook believed that a healthy soul for the Jewish nation could only be formed by drawing the two philosophies together. This became his lifelong project, to which he applied all the powers of his mystical imagination.

This mystical viewpoint was the centerpiece of his approach to everything, and it requires a brief explanation in order to make sense of Kook's understanding of *shmita*. Kook's religious study had introduced him to Lurianic Kabbalah, which most scholars hold to be the "backbone" of Kook's worldview.[7]

---

[5] According to Mirsky, the Old Yishuv was marked by two facets: "enthroning Torah study at the very pinnacle of religious life, and hastening the Messiah's advent by human action." See Mirsky, *Rav Kook,* 45.

[6] For an account of the various aspects of New Yishuv activism, see Mirsky, 46–47.

[7] See Julian Sinclair's introductory chapter, "Rav Kook and the Meaning of Shmita," in Kook, *Rav Kook's Introduction to Shabbat Ha'aretz,* 43.

This framework of Jewish mysticism is named after the distinguished Rabbi Isaac Luria (1534–72), who taught that the universe was pervaded with "sparks" of divine light which are the remnants of an explosive event at the beginning of creation.[8] According to Luria, infinite divine energy was poured into vessels that could not hold them and thus shattered.[9] Although the sparks can be found everywhere, they are usually shrouded by *kelipot*—shells of darkness that hide the divine energy. The aim of Jewish spirituality, in this paradigm, is to liberate the sparks. Because of the ubiquitous character of these sparks, anyone who seeks to unveil them must never hide from any source of spiritual truth, whether religious or secular.[10]

Kook applied the logic of this kabbalistic paradigm to his understanding of Jewish existence. The Jewish people, he believed, had the purpose of extending love to all people as part of the project of revealing divine light. This purpose entailed the rejection of a certain type of exclusive sovereignty:

---

[8] Luria's work builds on earlier forms of kabbalah based on the *Zohar* and the works of mystics such as Azriel of Gerona and Moses Cordovero. Isaac Luria himself wrote nothing, but his ideas were carried on through his disciples. For historical background descriptions of the kabbalah and specifically the Lurianic variety, see Daniel C. Matt, *The Essential Kabbalah: The Heart of Jewish Mysticism* (New York: HarperCollins, 1995). For a detailed account of Luria's life and work, see Lawrence Fine, *Physician of the Soul, Healer of the Cosmos: Isaac Luria and His Kabbalistic Fellowship* (Stanford, CA: Stanford University Press, 2003).

[9] For early accounts of this model of creation in the Lurianic Kabbalah, see Hayyim ben Joseph Vital, *Kabbalah of Creation: Isaac Luria's Earlier Mysticism,* trans. Eliahu Klein (North Vale, NJ: Jason Aronson Publications, 2000).

[10] As David Shatz observes, this hermeneutic of synthesis is central to Kook's approach to every aspect of theology. In a Jewish version of the Christian patristic idea of "plundering the Egyptians," Kook sought to derive the best aspects of any philosophy into his work. "Kook," Shatz notes, "exhorts Jews to open themselves to the realm of general culture, confronting and engaging the full range of secular teachings and disciplines." See David Shatz, *Jewish Thought in Dialogue: Essays on Thinkers, Theologies, and Moral Theories* (Boston: Academic Studies Press, 2009), 93.

As long as each one exalts himself, claiming I am sovereign, I and none other—there cannot be peace in our midst. . . . All our endeavors must be directed toward disclosing the light of general harmony, which derives not from suppressing any power, any thought, any tendency, but by bringing each of them within the vast ocean of light infinite, where all things find their unity, where all is ennobled, all is exalted, all is hallowed.[11]

Kook's kabbalistic mysticism directed him to frame every aspect of religious practice and teaching as a means toward harmony. For him, a genuine awareness of the divine sparks in all human beings must preclude a sense of opposition in human relationships. Simply put: Religion has a goal, which is the liberative harmony of all human beings.

This mystical attitude placed Kook in an odd place in the context of the debate over Jewish practice in Palestine. His position standing in the middle of Old and New Yishuvim was not a result of bland insouciance. He was not a mindless moderate. When it came to the importance of Jewish traditions, Kook sided wholly with the Old Yishuv, believing that a distinctly Jewish identity was crucial. Nevertheless, the reason why he believed in the preservation of the old rituals was that the distinct identity arising from them was precisely the means for creating a new, liberated humanity. Gershon Winer sums up the essence of this mentality, arguing that, for Kook, "Jewish nationalism is elevated to universal significance."[12] Kook did not believe that one should do Jewish rituals or

---

[11] Rav Kook, *Orot Hakodesh,* vol. II, 588, as cited in Ben Zion Bokser, "Introduction," in *Abraham Isaac Kook: The Lights of Penitence, the Moral Principles, Lights of Holiness, Essays, Letters, and Poems,* trans. Ben Zion Bokser (New York: Paulist Press, 1978), 8.

[12] Gershon Winer, "On Religious Nationalism," in *Essays on the Thought and Philosophy of Rabbi Kook,* ed. Ezra Gellman, 211–18 (New York: Cornwall Books, 2002), 215.

maintain a robust Jewish lifestyle just for the sake of being Jewish. Rather, the rituals were altruistic, aimed at liberating the divine light in all people.[13] Rituals were always *for something*. This practical mentality was what Kook believed the New Yishuv got right. It was also what ultimately led him to weigh in on one specific issue that divided the two communities, namely, *shmita*.

The *Shmita* Controversy

To understand the controversy that divided Jews in Jaffa, Palestine, when Rav Kook arrived there in 1904, we must step back and explain what *shmita* is, or was supposed to be. The first references to *shmita*—also called the sabbatical year—are found in Exodus and Leviticus. These passages articulate how the people of Israel should relate to the arable land they find when they enter Canaan:

> For six years you may sow your land and gather in its produce. But the seventh year you shall let it lie untilled and fallow, that the poor of your people may eat of it; and their leftovers the wild animals may eat. So also shall you do in regard to your vineyard, and your olive grove. (Ex 23:10–11)

Clearly, the purpose for this command is directly humanitarian: The land should not be cultivated "so that the poor of your

---

[13] David Shatz explains Kook's connection of Jewish nationalism with universalism in the following way: "Each nation has its distinctive talents, he explains; but the talent distinctive to the Jews is their capacity to absorb, synthesize, and transform the best elements in surrounding cultures. Israel is, thus, 'the quintessence of all humanity.' The mission of the Jews in history is to exercise their talent for integration and creativity and then to bring to the outside world the new product they have fashioned. Only in that way will Israel be able to execute its sacred task; to elevate all of humanity and all of existence" (Shatz, *Jewish Thought in Dialogue,* 93).

people may eat of it" along with the wild animals. A similar rationale is articulated in Leviticus 25, with an accent on God's possession of the land.[14] Of course, this raises numerous interpretive and historical questions. Specifically, how does not cultivating the land help the poor to have more food? One would assume that if the land were not cultivated, the poor would have *less* to eat rather than more. Such considerations have led scholars such as Leon Epsztein to posit that "the land could not have been left fallow. It was cultivated, but once the harvest was reaped, it was not taken in; the corn was left spread on the ground to be there for those who needed it."[15] Norman Habel disagrees, arguing that the text clearly points to a cessation of agriculture in every respect.[16] The latter position is also affirmed by John Dominic Crossan, who points out that Josephus records an absence of sowing in Israel during the seventh year.[17] Perhaps it is most likely that the intention of the command was for the rich owners of the land to give it over to the poor during the year—thus it would have not been formally cultivated but would still provide a source of food

---

[14] The Leviticus passage reads: "When you enter the land that I am giving you, let the land, too, keep a sabbath for the Lord. For six years you may sow your field, and for six years prune your vineyard, gathering in their produce. But during the seventh year the land shall have a sabbath of complete rest, a sabbath for the Lord, when you may neither sow your field nor prune your vineyard. The aftergrowth of your harvest you shall not reap, nor shall you pick the grapes of your untrimmed vines. It shall be a year of rest for the land. While the land has its sabbath, all its produce will be food to eat for you yourself and for your male and female slave, for your laborer and the tenant who live with you, and likewise for your livestock and for the wild animals on your land" (Lev 25:2–7).

[15] Leon Epsztein, *Social Justice in the Ancient Near East and the People of the Bible* (London: SCM Press, 1986), 132.

[16] See Norman Habel, *The Land Is Mine: Six Biblical Land Ideologies* (Minneapolis: Fortress Press, 1995), 103.

[17] John Dominic Crossan, *The Birth of Christianity* (New York: Harper Collins, 1999), 190. For Josephus's record of first-century *shmita* observance, see his *Jewish Antiquities,* 14:202.

for lower-class workers. Whatever the case may have been, we need only observe here that *shmita* emerged as a means of communal justice. The purpose of the command is to restore community by leveling inequality, both among humans and between humans and animals. This is an important point for understanding Kook's approach to *shmita*.

Among Jews not residing on land in Israel, *shmita* was not practiced. However, toward the end of the nineteenth century, when Jews began returning to Palestine and commencing agricultural activity, the question of how and whether to implement *shmita* became a central issue. This controversy over an ancient Jewish practice is the context in which Kook's contribution emerges.

The argument had kicked off in 1888, when the New Yishuv realized that their survival within the land of Israel depended on continuing to profit from the land during the sabbatical year. Obviously, anyone hoping to run a stable agricultural business cannot leave all land fallow every seventh year without facing significant income shortages. The New Yishuv asked several significant European rabbis (most notably Yitzak Spektor) about how to resolve the problem, and were given an ingenious workaround. The rabbis told the New Yishuv that it would be acceptable to profit from the land during the *shmita*, as long as it was sold to non-Jews.[18] At the end of the *shmita* year, the land would be sold back to the original Jewish owners at a modest

---

[18] More specifically, according to Michael Nehorai, the *heter mekhira* contained two stipulations: "(1) that the land be sold to a non-Jew by way of circumvention, as we are accustomed to do with unleavened bread on Passover; and (2) that all manner of agricultural work—to begin with—be done by non-Jews, and that even in a situation of duress all modes of work that are biblically prohibited should not be done by Jews." See Michael Z. Nehorai, "Halakhah, Metahalakha, and the Redemption of Israel: Reflections on the Rabbinic Rulings of Rav Kook," in *Rabbi Abraham Isaac Kook and Jewish Spirituality,* ed. Lawrence J. Kaplan and David Shatz (New York: New York University Press, 1995), 128.

gain to their non-Jewish partners.[19] In this way the Jewish landowners were technically not violating the *shmita* command, because they were not working "their" land during the *shmita* year. This compromise became known as the *heter mekhira.*

The traditional Old Yishuv sensed that this was an illegitimate loophole. After all, if I sell something to someone with the understanding that I will buy it back after a certain time, most people would say that I have not really sold it but only rented it out. Not surprisingly, then, the *heter mekhira* triggered caustic debates between the different Jewish communities. The Old Yishuv alleged that it was nothing more than a faithless abandonment of Jewish tradition, while the New Yishuv insisted that it was unavoidable if Jews wanted to maintain a space in the land.

The debate over the *heter mekhira* continued to grow in intensity every seven years, becoming especially vehement in 1909–10, when the Jewish agricultural establishments had grown in size and could by no means survive a complete cessation of labor for the entire year. It was in this context that Kook wrote his opinion on it.

Although Kook was a mystic and a passionate lover of Jewish rituals, he argued in favor of the *heter mekhira.* Kook openly admitted that this provision was innovative, without solid backing in Jewish norms. He also admitted that he had changed his mind—while living in Europe, Kook had initially

---

[19] As Asher Cohen and Bernard Susser observe, this meant that the sale of the land was essentially "fictitious," since the sale involved an agreement that the land would be bought back after the *shmita* year. On the technicalities of this process, see Asher Cohen and Bernard Susser, "The 'Sabbatical' Year in Israeli Politics: An Intra-Religious and Religious-Secular Conflict from the Nineteenth through the Twenty-First Centuries," *Journal of Church and State* 52, no. 3 (2010): 454–75. The fictitious nature of the *heter mekhira* is part of what made the practice so controversial among more traditional Jewish settlers in the land of Israel.

opposed the *heter mekhira.*[20] Why, then, did Kook now support it? Was it because he had lost faith in the importance of the *shmita* ritual? On the contrary, Kook argued that it was precisely because of his value of *shmita* that he believed it should be suspended. The argument he made is both fascinating and insightful for thinking about the nature of inoperativity.

Kook's Argument for the *Heter Mekhira*

Kook's case for compromising on *shmita* begins rather strangely. Instead of arguing that the *shmita* is an outdated practice no longer relevant to the modern world, Kook extols the ritual, claiming that its practice is part of the heartbeat of Jewish existence. The *shmita*, he says, is just as important for Judaism as the weekly Sabbath: "What the Sabbath does for the individual, Shmita does for the nation as a whole."[21] In the modern world, Kook says, the *shmita* is more necessary than ever, because of our production-oriented, *homo faber* mentality. The ritual enables us to see beyond this mentality and grasp our basic human identity. Kook explains:

> On the shmita, our pure, inner spirit may be revealed as it truly is. The forcefulness that is inevitably part of our regular, public lives lessens our moral refinement. There is always a tension between the ideal of listening to the voice inside us that calls us to be kind, truthful, and merciful, and the conflict, compulsion, and pressure to be unyielding that surround buying, selling, and acquiring things. These aspects of the world of action distance us

---

[20] See Daniel Z. Feldman, "A Brief Overview of Some of the Issues Related to the *Hetter Mekhira,*" *Tradition* 47, no. 3 (2014): 9. Feldman emphasizes that it was Kook's relocation to the land of Israel that facilitated his change of thought on this issue.

[21] Kook, *Rav Kook's Introduction to Shabbat Ha'aretz,* 95.

from the divine light and prevent its being discerned in the public life of the nation.[22]

Keep in mind that in Kook's kabbalistic mysticism the "pure, inner spirit" is the essence of the divine sparks. Its qualities are those of God. The style of existence displayed in *shmita*, therefore, reveals God, and the celebrants of *shmita* model the divine existence through the ritual. *Shmita* would transform their souls after the divine pattern.

Part of the value of *shmita*, according to Kook, is precisely that it is a religious ritual. In a way that prefigures Pieper's claim that only a religious "feast" can bring about true leisure, Kook argues that a "pervasive divine perspective that rests in the spirit of the people" is impossible in "a way of life that is purely secular."[23] Kook claims that the inoperativity of *shmita* is essential because the modern secular life, "full of frenetic action, veils the glory of our divine soul, and the soul's clear light is blocked from shining through the overpowering, mundane reality."[24] Certainly no one can dispute Kook's commitment to the value of *shmita*. He believes it will be celebrated in full, in the future. But not yet.

If *shmita* is effective in changing the soul of the people, why not start observing it right away? Why permit the *heter mekhira* to hamper the people's embrace of godliness, preventing the transformative effects of this inoperative ritual? Kook's answer is that doing so would destroy the original purpose of the *shmita*, which was to restore the people's connection to the land and create community. Because of economic circumstances, the rabbis who instituted the *heter mekhira* "realized their historical obligation to smooth the path of the new settlements and, as much as possible, not to let the *mitzvot* [commands] that are

---

[22] Kook, 96–97.

[23] Kook, 93.

[24] Kook, 93.

connected to the land be obstacles."[25] If the *shmita* was a suspension of activity to make way for life, in this case the people
needed a "suspension of the suspension" in order to fulfill the
intent of *shmita*. This dynamic is precisely what Agamben calls
the "messianic" inoperativity. For Kook, the only way to preserve the goal of *shmita* is to cancel the sovereignty of *shmita*.

Against the traditionalists who believed all Jews had an
obligation to literally observe *shmita* exactly as depicted in the
Torah, Kook pointed out that the provision was necessary for
the survival of the agricultural industries for poor Jews in Palestine. At bottom, the debate was less about *shmita* specifically
and more about the legitimacy of the secular Jews who formed
the greater part of the New Yishuv. If they could not profit from
the land during the *shmita* year, Kook observed, they would
find their very existence jeopardized. Although his traditional
sympathies were with the Old Yishuv, Kook approached the
New Yishuv with a mentality informed by his kabbalistic pre-
dispositions. Kook believed that there were sparks of divine
holiness in these secular Jews even though they were lax in
their ritual observance, and this divine essence must be allowed
to emerge. Ousting them from the holy land by forbidding them
an essential compromise with the *shmita* mandate would only
set back the progress of the divine light.

Kook also argued that mandating full observance of the
shmita would directly harm the least fortunate Jews, thus con-
tradicting the original purpose of the ritual. In Kook's time it
would have been impossible for anyone but the wealthy pioneers in the land of Israel to practice *shmita*.[26] For Kook, the

---

[25] Kook, 137.

[26] Feldman sees in Kook's defense of the *heter mekhira* a concern to
prevent something like a spiritual inequality emerging in the land of Israel.
Wealthy farmers would have spiritual access to the soul-reviving powers of
shmita, because they could afford to take a year off. On the other hand, "on
a spiritual level, there is the concern that non-observant farmers will cease
to have any connection to shemitta, were the hetter to be unavailable." See

mystical goal of rituals was restoring the soul of the people, and this could only happen by drawing rich and poor together into the spirit of the ritual. By making the practice of the ritual contingent on the financial ability of all the Jews in the land, and simultaneously working for the eventual restoration of *shmita* observance, Kook essentially argued for a campaign for economic equality. In a manner that parallels the Christian "preferential option for the poor," Kook's *shmita* posited a key principle of messianic inoperativity—it must be accessible to everyone. No one truly rests if the "poor of the land" cannot eat.

Another reason why Kook supported the *heter mekhira* because of the mystical principles of *shmita* was that the practice of "selling" the land during the ritual year brought Jews and non-Jews into mutual harmony. In Kook's kabbalistic framework, rituals must elicit the freedom of the mystical sparks in the global community—and these sparks burn brightest when the flames merge together. Hence, according to one scholar, Kook promoted the *heter mekhira* as a way to draw non-Jews and secular Zionists into a collaboration—one that would eventually result in a full observance of *shmita*.[27] For the *heter mekhira* to work, Jews had to deliberately help non-Jews with their agricultural industries (by allowing them to work the land for the *shmita* year) and non-Jews had to intentionally support Jews in the partial observance of their religious ritual. The suspension of the ritual thus paradoxically fulfilled the mystical intent of the ritual, which was greater flourishing of humanity, achieved by unity in diversity.

Feldman, "A Brief Overview of Some of the Issues Related to the *Hetter Mekhira*," 27.

[27] Shemesh points out that Kook's concern for Muslims and a desire to draw them into mutual community in the land of Israel could also have been a factor in his promotion of the *heter mekhira*. See Abraham Ofir Shemesh, "'For the Public's Improvement and for the Benefit of the Town': Correspondence between the Rabbi Kook and Residents of the Moshavot in Eretz Israel on Ecological and Environmental Matters," *Modern Judaism* 38, no. 1 (2018): 59.

Kook's vision of interreligious harmony was not based on mere "toleration" between religious groups. A tolerance approach often promotes hiding religious and ethnic identities or relegating them to the periphery of human affairs. Kook's approach was the opposite of this. His ideal was for religious identity to foster active support among persons of different faiths. Kook posited that being Jewish and practicing Jewish rituals did not signal that a person was "against" or even indifferent to other communities, but was—through the ritual identity—intentionally liberating the divine soul in all humanity. The *heter mekhira* provided a way for a ritual that affirmed a specific religious embodiment (being Jewish) to bring a universal benefit to humanity. Paradoxically, when it came to a ritual like *shmita*, "not doing" was the best way to "do."

A final reason Kook defended a compromise on *shmita* observance was that he recognized a fascinating element of genuine inoperativity in rituals: It cannot be coercively imposed. Once again, Kook did not arrive at this principle through a standard modern tolerance impulse. His idea was not "let people do whatever they want because it does not matter." The origins of his belief in noncoercion were emphatically mystical. "God," Kook wrote, "does not make tyrannical and unreasonable demands of His creatures."[28] At the root of the traditionalists' insistence on rigid adherence to the *shmita* mandate was a failure to understand the sovereignty of the God who gave the mandate. The inoperativity of *shmita* must arise from the authority of a deity who mystically transforms the soul rather than coercively commands it. As Tamar Ross notes, this same mystical idea of "the intrinsic value of noncoercion" was evident in other policies Kook commended, such as his methods of addressing religiously heterodox members of the community.[29]

---

[28] Kook, *Rav Kook's Introduction to Shabbat Ha'aretz,* 137.

[29] Ross analyzes Kook's various statements encouraging toleration for nonbelievers and "heretics" in the land of Israel, finding that Kook's toleration was grounded in his mystical approach to *halacha.* According to Ross, Kook

The kabbalistic idea of sparks within each person that need only to be flamed into action sets the stage for a mode of interpersonal ethics in which "letting be" becomes the paradigm for politics as a whole.

Paradoxically, Kook argued that the lack of observance of *shmita* can be a way to preserve its memory and significance. "Since the evasion is carried out according to the prescriptions of the law, it constitutes a remembrance of the precept so that the law will not be forgotten, and when the time comes again for them to observe the biblical law, all the laws will be known."[30] The point was to study and celebrate the principles of *shmita*, as well as enact any parts of the relevant *halakha* that were within the grasp of possibility. Doing so would gradually renovate the vitality of the collective Jewish soul, making possible a progressively greater celebration of *shmita*. The Jewish people should not treat *shmita* as a dogmatic dictate that must be served as if it were a slavemaster. The *shmita* was made for the goal of liberation, thus the people should—in this case—liberate themselves from it, temporarily.[31]

This notion that inoperativity has a "goal" points to the first half of the paradox we noted at the beginning of this chapter.

---

believed that "although the natural instinct of the national spirit is to assert its authority whenever signs of spiritual disintegration become apparent, such authority can be effectively imposed only when the nation's powers are at the height of their perfection." See Tamara Ross, "Between Metaphysical and Liberal Pluralism: A Reappraisal of Rabbi A. I. Kook's Espousal of Toleration," *Association for Jewish Studies Review* 21, no. 1 (1996): 81.

[30] Kook, *Rav Kook's Introduction to Shabbat Ha'aretz,* 45.

[31] This did not mean that settlers in the land of Israel *must* utilize the *heter mekhira.* As Simcha Raz notes, Kook "made sure that those farmers who wanted to adhere to the laws of *Shemittah* would be able to do so, not letting anyone force them to rely on the *heter.* He even urged farmers to refrain from working the land, if they could afford to do so, and he set up a special fund to assist them." See Simcha Raz, *Angel among Men: Impressions from the Life of Avraham Yitzchak Hakohen Kook* (Jerusalem: Kol Mevaser Publications, 2003), 31.

Kook's work indicates that true, liberative inoperativity is a steppingstone rather than an obstacle to human flourishing. Kook's approach to *shmita* is parallel to Jesus's approach to Sabbath in the first century (which was not different from that of many Jewish rabbis at the time): "The Sabbath was made for man; not man for the Sabbath" (Mk 2:27). Divorcing ritual inoperativity from its humanistic goals will woefully lead to the type of sovereign stasis Agamben warned us about, in which humans find their liberty and agency swallowed by a mechanistic system. It will also lead to a scenario in which humans can observe a ritual, and then go forth and subjugate or massacre one another.

The most significant aspect of Kook's argument regarding the *heter mekhira*, however, is that he points toward a stunning possibility that will be crucial for developing an ethics of inoperative rituals, that is, such rituals must practically extend beyond themselves, affecting domains of life that seem irreligious. Kook believed that the principle of *shmita* was not simply to live one year without agriculture. Rather, it was to create a society of rest. This meant that the practice of *shmita* could involve and even command doing things like agricultural cooperation and business deals. This suggests that perhaps all inoperative rituals must break the bonds of sacrality. If a ritual like *shmita* (and also Sabbath, prayer, or vigil) points to a God of liberative inoperativity, this ritual *cannot* be a discrete event, because God cannot be bounded by any sacral categories. If the ritual does not affect the whole of life (including politics and economics), it is not a genuine ritual of inoperativity. The boundaries of inoperative rituals must always be porous.

Perhaps the reader might have an objection to Kook's "instrumental" framing of inoperative rituals, asking if he reduces inoperativity to a humanistic tool. If we simply say "inoperativity has a goal," we make inoperative rituals a means for accomplishing something, and thus their status as "doing nothing" appears to vanish. We need to explore the second half of the paradox and then try to figure out how inoperativity both "functions" and does nothing simultaneously. For this task, Catholic theologian Roberto Goizueta can help us.

Roberto Goizueta: Doing Nothing Is Useless

Like Kook, Goizueta writes from the perspective of a community that has faced marginalization and displacement. Goizueta's scholarship explores the experiences of Latinx communities in the United States, who, despite being "Americans" and officially practicing the dominant religion of the North American continent, often find themselves in a precarious position. Facing language discrimination, racism, cultural stereotypes, and a relentless interrogation of their "status," these communities seek out ways to preserve their life together through rituals—some of which are specifically religious, while others appear at the margins of this designation. Although his analysis appears in a similar setting to Kook's, Goizueta's exploration of these rituals shows the flip side of Kook's insistence that inoperative rituals must accomplish something.

But before explaining Goizueta's understanding of rituals in the Latinx context, it is first vital to explain Goizueta's focus on Latinx "popular religion" and what it involves.

Latinx Popular Religion

Any reference to popular religion may be likely to evoke images of commercialized, reckless, naive forms of spirituality, perhaps as contrasted with supposedly more serious "academic" religion. Goizueta's use of the term does not correspond to such pejorative assumptions. Goizueta points out that all religious reflections result from dialogue with personal background and life experiences, and that no theologian can interpret a doctrine or text apart from these personal factors.[32] In a sense, then, because of its emergence within the framework of culture, all religious study is popular. In Goizueta's case, his work is a reflection of his own experience within the specific setting of US Latinx culture.

What then, is Latinx popular religion? As a precise term, *popular religion* is difficult to define—a challenge Goizueta understands.[33] At first the term can seem to indicate religion that is popular in the sense of common, well liked, or trendy, in a way analogous to "popular music." This is not the sense in which Goizueta uses the term. The popular religious elements in Latinx Catholicism can be either widespread or parochial, and may be well known or somewhat hidden. For example, devotion to the Virgin of Guadalupe is not popular in the sense that it is universally known (many of my students at a Catholic university have not even heard of this devotion), but it is popular because it is central to the lives of everyday people in specific religious settings. In Goizueta's theology, therefore, "the adjective [*popular*] refers to the socio-historical fact that these religious symbols, practices, and narratives are *of the people.*"[34] In other words, the popular religion of Latinx Catholicism emerges directly out of the common experiences of marginalized and diverse communities.

What makes Latinx popular religion significant, according to Goizueta, is the importance of sacramentality within its theological framework. The term *sacramentality* here does not pertain specifically to the sacraments of Christianity (although

---

[32] See Roberto Goizueta, *Caminemos con Jesús: Toward a Hispanic/Latino Theology of Accompaniment* (Maryknoll, NY: Orbis Books, 1995), 10.

[33] Goizueta discusses the difficulty of defining popular religion (Goizueta, 20–27). On this challenge, see also Orlando Espín, "Popular Catholicism among Latinos," in *Hispanic Catholicism in the United States: Issues and Concerns,* ed. P. Dolan and Allan Figueroa Deck (Notre Dame, IN: University of Notre Dame Press, 1994); and Robert J. Schreiter, *Constructing Local Theologies* (Maryknoll, NY: Orbis Books, 1985), 122–43.

[34] Goizueta, *Caminemos con Jesús,* 21.

it includes these), but more broadly to the idea that God may be experienced *within* actions, events, and rituals. Someone with a sacramental mindset, in this sense, will not engage in a ritual and think merely about what its doctrinal implications are. For example, such a person will not eat the bread of the Eucharist and think abstractly, "I am doing this because I will receive the grace of Christ as a result of doing it." The sacramentally minded person would not deny this theological statement, but would find it odd. The reason for this oddness would be that such a doctrinal or theological explanation seems to imply that the bread of the Eucharist is a steppingstone to something else, or a tool. By contrast, the sacramental worshipper would find the importance or significance of the ritual contained within the ritual. A sacramental framework sees grace *in the ritual of eating the bread.* In this sense, sacramental and inoperative are nearly synonymous.

Why is Latinx Christianity more apt to be sacramental in character? Goizueta points to the research of scholars such as Orlando Espín and Mark Francis, who have shown that the Catholicism of Latinx Catholics emerged historically from Iberian traditions that predated modern Catholicism. This type of Catholicism was more "medieval" in character, which means that it did not display the focus on conceptual and doctrinal specificity that characterized the Catholicism of the Counter-Reformation.[35] Unlike some other forms of Catholicism, Iberian tradition lacked a need to explain or justify its practices in utilitarian terms. As a result, for many traditional Latinx

---

[35] On this, see Orlando Espín, *Faith of the People: Theological Reflections on Popular Catholicism* (Maryknoll, NY: Orbis Books, 1997), 117; Orlando Espín, "Pentecostalism and Popular Catholicism: The Poor and *Traditio,*" *Journal of Hispanic/Latino Theology* 3, no. 2 (November 1995): 19; and Mark Francis, "Popular Piety and Liturgical Reform in a Hispanic Context," in *Dialogue Rejoined: Theology and Ministry in the United States Hispanic Reality*, ed. Ana María Pineda and Robert Schreiter (Collegeville, MN: Liturgical Press, 1995), 165–66.

Christians, rituals are less like creeds that must be defended and more like family members—you do not ask why someone is your family member or analyze them in order to prove their value; you simply accept them as integral to your life.[36] This basic framework is crucial to Goizueta's analysis of rituals.

Goizueta's approach to Latinx popular religion is also closely tied to the framework of Latin American liberation theology—the movement of theologians in the 1960s and 1970s who argued that God cannot be understood apart from efforts to systemically uplift and empower the poor. As we will see, Goizueta affirms much of liberation theology, but he also tries to correct certain deficiencies in it. On the positive side, Goizueta lauds the basic liberation theology concept that Christ is present within the faith of the poor. "For Christians," Goizueta says, "the significance of the crucified and risen Christ is precisely that God is found, in some special way, among those people who continue to be crucified today—the poor, the hungry, the naked, and the outcast."[37] To understand the presence of God in the world, we should look at the lives of these people. Gustavo Gutiérrez formulated this method in liberation theology by claiming that theology is a "critical reflection on praxis" and that theology could only be verified by "orthopraxis."[38]

---

[36] Goizueta argues that within the devotional framework of Latinx popular religion, practices are embedded within a community's social and religious life. These practices are seen as "giving" life to the community. This helps to prevent the type of "shopping around" for religious practices that makes them expendable carriers of meaning. The rituals of Latinx Catholicism thus have a deep connection to the enchanted world of medieval Catholicism which much of Northern-European and American Catholicism has lost, largely as a result of nominalism. See Roberto Goizueta, *Christ Our Companion: Toward a Theological Aesthetics of Liberation* (Maryknoll, NY: Orbis Books, 2009), 72–84. See also Vincent J. Miller, *Consuming Religion: Christian Faith and Practice in a Consumer Culture* (New York: Continuum, 2004).

[37] Roberto Goizueta, "Love the Poor You're With: The Editors Interview Roberto S. Goizueta," *US Catholic* (August 1, 2013): 26–30, 29.

[38] See Gustavo Gutiérrez, *A Theology of Liberation* (Maryknoll, NY: Orbis Books, 1973), 6–15, 45. For an expanded theological work also based on this

Goizueta agrees with this statement, but he thinks it needs further elaboration and clarification by looking more closely at the lives of marginalized persons themselves. This is where his views on the nature of inoperativity become important.

Praxis and the Useless Fiesta

If we follow liberation theology and affirm that the heart of Christian faith and theology is praxis, we are faced with an obvious and yet difficult question that Goizueta poses: "What is praxis?"[39] Both liberation theologians and their critics often assume that praxis is simply "doing something," and that the point is to figure out how to do it. But Goizueta argues that this level of analysis is insufficient, because there are a variety of ways of understanding what *doing* means.

Goizueta observes that Karl Marx, whose work has had some influence on liberation theology, defined praxis as making or production—useful activity. This type of activity is the central hallmark of human nature. "In creating an objective world by his practical activity, in working-up inorganic nature, man proves himself a conscious species being," Marx says.[40] By production, human beings give form to substances and concomitantly give form to themselves.[41] The result is that, when

---

principle, see Juan Luis Segundo, *The Liberation of Theology* (Maryknoll, NY: Orbis Books, 1976). For an overview of the primacy of praxis in liberation theology, see Alfred T. Hennelly, *Liberation Theologies: The Global Pursuit of Justice* (Mystic, CT: Twenty-Third Publications, 1995).

[39] Goizueta, *Caminemos con Jesús*, 80.

[40] Karl Marx, "Economic and Philosophic Manuscripts of 1844," in *The Marx-Engels Reader,* ed. Robert C. Tucker (New York: W. W. Norton, 1978), 76, as cited in Goizueta, *Caminemos con Jesús,* 81.

[41] Marx puts it very straightforwardly: "He [the human being] begins to distinguish himself from the animal the moment he begins to produce his means of subsistence, a step required by his physical organization. By producing food, man indirectly produces his material life itself." See Karl Marx, *Writings of the Young Marx on Philosophy and Society,* ed. Loyd Easton and Kurt Guddat (Garden City, NY: Doubleday, 1967), 409, as cited in Goizueta, *Caminemos con Jesús,* 81.

human beings produce goods to be sold on the market, the very selves of the producers are being sold. This is the core of what Marx famously calls alienation.[42] Implicit, then, within Marx's critique of capitalist structures is an anthropology in which "the human person is *homo faber.*"[43]

Although Marx vehemently opposed alienation, he did not question the Enlightenment concept of praxis on which it was based. In fact, he insisted that the point of his philosophy was to create change—to "produce" a society with different distribution structures. According to Goizueta, Marx could not avoid the influence of production-oriented thinking, even in his opposition to the inevitable exploitation that resulted from such thinking. The same outcome arises for liberation theologians influenced by Marx. Although Goizueta agrees with the work of pivotal figures such as Gustavo Gutiérrez and the Boff brothers, Leonardo and Clodovis, in restoring the primacy of praxis into Christian theology, he argues that this concept has been built from an Enlightenment utility mold. Liberation theology, by focusing on transforming the world, runs the danger of assuming that human beings are defined by their capacity to effect changes in sociopolitical systems. A religion based on critical reflection on praxis—when praxis is defined this way—will be a religion of production and making, and will reduce human

---

[42] On the concept of alienation, see Marx, "Economic and Philosophical Manuscripts of 1844," XXIII (in the chapter "Estranged Labor"). See also Nicholas Churchich, *Marxism and Alienation* (Rutherford, NJ: Fairleigh Dickinson University Press, 1990); V. V. Ivanchuk, "Alienation and the Project of Man's Universal Emancipation in Early Marx," *Grani* 20, no. 3 (2017): 98–103; Chris Byron, "Essence and Alienation: Marx's Theory of Human Nature," *Science and Society* 80, no. 3 (2016): 375–94.

[43] Goizueta, *Caminemos con Jesús,* 82. To make this observation, Goizueta draws on Kostas Axelos, *Alienation, Praxis, and Techne in the Thought of Karl Marx* (Austin: University of Texas Press, 1976). Goizueta also employs a critique of Marx's utilitarian anthropology found in Hannah Arendt, *The Human Condition* (Chicago: University of Chicago Press, 1958).

beings to the type of sovereignly controlled mechanisms that Agamben warns us about.

However, according to Goizueta, this definition of praxis as production is not the only definition available. Goizueta points to Aristotle, who makes a key distinction between *praxis* and *poiesis.* The latter term refers to production or making— "human action whose end is *external* to itself."[44] Praxis, for Aristotle, refers to behavior aimed at internal ends—that is, action done for its own sake.[45] Goizueta uses several analogies to illustrate the difference between praxis and poiesis. Someone who *makes* a guitar engages in poiesis, because the object created is intended for another purpose (playing music). Someone who *plays* the guitar, on the other hand, engages in praxis, because the act of musical production is an end in itself (unless, of course, the player attempts to use the guitar music only to accomplish some other end, such as earning money). Another, subtler analogy Goizueta uses is the distinction between "making a house" and "making a home." Someone who fits boards together creates a space that will be used for another purpose: living. This externally oriented act is poiesis. However, the persons who eat, sleep, and enjoy themselves within the house engage in praxis. Their living is an end in itself.[46]

Modern Western society, in Goizueta's evaluation, has largely neglected Aristotle's definition of life as praxis in favor of the Enlightenment perspective of life as production—the view that Marx also adopted. The result has been a tendency to

---

[44] Goizueta, *Caminemos con Jesús,* 83.

[45] Goizueta draws this distinction from an analysis of Aristotle's *Politics,* 1.4.1254, and his *Nicomachean Ethics,* 6.4.1140. See Goizueta, *Caminemos con Jesús,* 83nn12–14.

[46] Goizueta, *Caminemos con Jesús,* 83. Goizueta draws the latter analogy from Nicholas Lobkowicz, *Theory and Practice: History of a Concept from Aristotle to Marx* (Notre Dame, IN: University of Notre Dame Press, 1967), 10.

instrumentalize human persons, to depict their value in terms of their ability to transform their world.

Goizueta affirms the importance of transforming the world. But his recognition of the subtle instrumental anthropology lurking within liberation theology leads him to the following critique:

> My own experience in Latino communities, such as San Fernando, has also led me to question . . . any emphasis on the social transformative dimension of human action which would make this dimension itself foundational. In these communities, I have witnessed a type of empowerment and liberation taking place which, at least initially and explicitly, seems to have relatively little connection to any social or political struggles. Indeed, in many cases, empowerment and liberation are not explicit goals at all. Seemingly, the only explicit goals are day-to-day survival and, especially, the affirmation of relationships as essential to that survival. This affirmation is manifested in all those seemingly insignificant ways in which we love, care for, and embrace other persons. Central to the struggle for survival and relationships, moreover, is the community's life of faith, which also, at least on the surface, seems little related to social transformation.[47]

The key point here is not to exclude transformation of society as a goal, but to look beyond that goal. What is the point of making a better society? Goizueta is highlighting a truth that many suffering, marginalized communities have recognized: Life itself needs to be lived for its own sake. Transformation has value, but inordinate emphasis on transformation can conceal the importance of what is transformed.

The idea of life together as an end in itself is the foundation for Goizueta's exploration of the rituals and celebrations

---

[47] Goizueta, *Caminemos con Jesús,* 88.

of popular Catholicism, which could otherwise be derided as useless folk tradition. Participants in a *via dolorosa* reenactment, for example, do not follow the footsteps of Christ in order to accomplish something, such as illustrating the liberative significance of the cross. Their action does not have a transformative "reason" attached to it.[48] Granted, a *via dolorosa* procession in a Latinx community may have the byproduct of signaling a theopolitical point—such as Christ's presence with the "crucified people" of history[49]—and thus contribute directly to transforming the world. But this is not the focus. The ritual aims at nothing other than itself. Such activities are intended to draw the participant into a physical, tangible relationship to God and community, and thus construct an intrinsically good concrete way of being in the world.

This inoperative quality to Latinx Catholic ritual becomes even clearer in an essay Goizueta writes on Latinx celebrative practices, or fiesta.[50] How does a fiesta establish a socially transformative and yet useless praxis? Goizueta answers this question by giving a detailed explanation of the philosophy of fiesta. He begins apophatically. "The fiesta," Goizueta writes, "is *not* a party."[51] Although the fiesta does involve pure enjoyment, displayed in merriment of various kinds (music, food,

---

[48] Speaking of a participant in one of these reenactments, Goizueta sums up his point: "God is revealed in the doing, in the active participation, in the hammering of the nails. It is in the act of walking alongside Jesus and all the others on the Via Dolorosa, and in the act of hammering the nails into Jesus' feet, that this man encounters God—in the most concrete, physical way possible. The only end, or goal, of the man's action is simply the action itself" (Goizueta, 103).

[49] For the thinking of Ignacio Ellacuría in regard to this phrase, see Ignacio Ellacuría, *Ignacio Ellacuría: Essays on History, Liberation, and Salvation* (Maryknoll, NY: Orbis Books, 2013).

[50] Roberto Goizueta, "Fiesta: Life in the Subjunctive," in *From the Heart of Our People: Latino/a Explorations in Catholic Systematic Theology,* ed. Orlando Espín and Miguel Diaz (Maryknoll, NY: Orbis Books, 1999), 84–99.

[51] Goizueta, 90.

and dancing), it is also a serious ontological reality. It is a way of being together as a community—not simply a way to fulfill oneself as an individual partier. As Goizueta puts it, "The fiesta is, at the same time, play *and* work."[52]

The work that is part of a fiesta is not merely the physical labor involved in setting up the amenities for revelry. It is the aspect of intentional community construction involved in the recreation. Goizueta points to research done by Ronald Grimes on the fiestas of Santa Fe, in which participants were asked if they could use music other than mariachi for the events. The response was emphatic: "The fiesta would no longer be a fiesta."[53] The quintessence of the fiesta is creating and drawing together a community, and this requires culturally authentic elements—in this case, mariachi rhythms. This authenticity is part of the identity of a fiesta.

At the same time, Goizueta says, a fiesta is not work defined as production. Using Aristotelian terminology, it is *praxis*, not *poiesis*. According to Goizueta, the inherent "uselessness" of this praxis enables those who participate in the fiesta to experience life as a gift, not a human-made construct. Goizueta points out that when Latinx communities celebrate in the face of adversity,

> what we are receiving and responding to is the gift of life, not in a sentimental sense, but in an ontological sense: we know that whatever "we" do, make or achieve is ultimately gift; we know that whatever relationships we construct are grounded in the prior constitutive relationship with the One who has loved us first; we know that who we are is not dependent on what we do, make,

---

[52] Goizueta, 91.

[53] Ronald Grimes, *Symbol and Conquest: Public Ritual and Drama in Santa Fe, New Mexico* (Ithaca, NY: Cornell University Press, 1976), 194, as cited in Goizueta, "Fiesta," 92.

or achieve; we know that life—all of life—is *gift* before
it is an "object" that we work upon, mold, transform, or
liberate.[54]

In this mindset any attempt to accomplish a "goal" or serve
some higher purpose through fiesta would be wrongheaded.
Fiesta rituals accomplish nothing, and trying to make them do
so would be to understand them wrongly.

Why does Goizueta strongly resist the idea that fiesta rituals
may be productive or useful? As María Dávila observes, Goizueta's aim is to analyze and expose "the elements in Western
capitalist societies that promote an irrational individualist and
consumerist self-identity that is counter-relational."[55] The
market system can surreptitiously seep into every element of
celebration in American culture, slowly transforming rituals
such as holidays, family get-togethers, and other forms of
celebration into tools for worshipping the economic system.
These are the faux festivals that Pieper warned about, and they
impose themselves easily in the realm of recreation. Faux, commercialized festivals, in Agamben's terms, force human beings
into machine-like "bare life" roles, depriving them of genuine
personhood. Goizueta's solution for resisting the hegemony of
commercialism is not to push back by sheer force of will or
an ascetic mentality, but to incarnate a different attitude, one
that deliberately insists on doing nothing. This inoperativity is
the basis for whatever other "activism" proceeds later on. As
Goizueta puts it, "The seedbed of all ethical-political action is
the basic affirmation: I AM A PERSON . . . or, more accurately,
WE ARE PERSONS . . . WE ARE A PEOPLE!"[56]

---

[54] Goizueta, 95–96.
[55] María Teresa Dávila, "A 'Preferential Option': A Challenge to Faith in
a Culture of Privilege," in *The Word Became Culture,* ed. Miguel H. Díaz
(Maryknoll, NY: Orbis Books, 2020), 63.
[56] Goizueta, *Caminemos con Jesús,* 130.

Synthesis

We now have the two sides of the inoperativity paradox in place. Kook claims that rituals such as *shmita* should serve a purpose. Goizueta claims that the ritual of fiesta is essentially useless. Now we need to explain how these two affirmations can be held simultaneously.

The key to uniting these two perspectives emerges in a phrase Goizueta uses to describe fiesta. He calls it "life in the subjunctive." Quoting Victor Turner, Goizueta suggests that during the fiesta, "it is as though everything is switched into the subjunctive mood for a privileged period of time."[57] The subjunctive is a grammatical term that applies more frequently in Spanish than in English; hence, it is possible that Latinx communities are more aware of its reality and significance. What Goizueta means by this term is a framework in which hope enters the present through an "as if" mentality. This mindset is not a matter of faking happiness where there is none or "playing pretend." Rather, as Ramon Luzarraga explains, the fiesta "declares that the daily challenges and misery of life will not have the last word; but the maintenance of Latino/a identity as a people beloved of God will."[58] By celebrating the subjunctive as the pinnacle "real" element of life, the fiesta is an ontological act whereby a new form of life arises. This is why Goizueta insists that fiesta is not an escape from the demands of the present or simply a distraction. Fiesta seeks to reverse the entire categories that we impose regarding ritual life and real life, by which we blindly assume that rituals are less real than normal life. Fiesta declares that normal, oppressive life is the fake; the celebration is the real.

---

[57] See Victor Turner, *The Anthropology of Performance* (New York: PAJ Publications, 1986), 128, as cited in Goizueta, "Fiesta," 93.

[58] Ramon Luzarraga, "Fiesta," in *Hispanic American Religious Cultures,* ed. Miguel De La Torre (Santa Barbara, CA: ABC CLIO, 2009), 265.

A close reading of Rav Kook's work reveals that this subjunctive mentality is what his mystical *heter mekhira* was also supposed to create. Just as Latinx communities in the United States cannot immediately and forcefully create a life free of discrimination, hierarchy, and poverty, the Jews living in Kook's Jaffa could not immediately spend a year of celebration and rest from working the land. However, they could—through the joyful partial suspension of *shmita*—bring the future eschatological reality of inoperativity into the present. Kook's *heter mekhira* was thus an act of "as if" living, a statement of hope in which Jews could affirm that a world of interreligious harmony, ecological prosperity, and peaceful agriculture was the true world, and that such a world would come to fruition.

Kook did not argue that *shmita* was only a tool for producing a new form of life. Rather, *shmita* was the key element in that life—one which needed to be suspended in order to be fulfilled. This point harmonizes perfectly with Goizueta's argument that inoperative ritual needs to be identified with life itself. In both perspectives the end result is a framework in which particular practices embody the type of identity Agamben calls "bios"— the life of humans freely relating to one another. For both Kook and Goizueta, human beings attain this life by adopting Agamben's *hos me*—"as not"—approach to their own lives, rituals, and communities. *Heter mekhira* and fiesta suspend the sovereignty of laws and regulations in order to allow a different but more real world to break into existence.

The primary difference between Kook's and Goizueta's approaches is that the sovereignty they oppose comes from different angles. In Kook's case, the danger lurked in a form of religious mechanization that insisted that rituals be observed in a rigid, uniform manner. Goizueta, by contrast, warns against a utilitarian, market-based thinking that would reduce rituals to goal-oriented commodities. These two dangers may seem antithetical, but a close examination shows them to be different flavors of the same cocktail. As Walter Benjamin argued, the market system is a "purely cultic (ritualized) religion, perhaps the most extreme that ever existed."[59] Agamben analyzes the hegemony of sovereign power from a traditional religious angle (the all-powerful God who demands submission), but the same insights could apply to the economic sphere (the all-powerful dollar). Both traditional religious and economic sovereignties seek to reduce human life to a means to an end. Kook and Goizueta push back against both of them.

We can thus return to the logical paradox of doing nothing in rituals: Inoperativity is inherently valuable and has no purpose outside of itself, but it also must have effects and purposes outside of itself. The resolution to this paradox appears when we realize that doing nothing can be truly pointless and transformational simultaneously, as long as it is understood as a form of life rather than as an artificial religious or economic distraction. Kook's and Goizueta's vision offers an additional layer of depth to the hackneyed phrase "Be the change you want to see in the world." In Kook's case we might rephrase this: "Be a Jewish community whose authentic rituals liberate the sparks of the world." In Goizueta's case: "Be a Latinx people whose joyous celebration models the value of all human life." Both of these imperatives are a form of doing nothing—and thus doing something.

The reason we must understand this paradox correctly if we want to develop an ethics of inoperativity is that it makes rituals much more than tasks we check off our "to do" list. It makes them recipes for life. Embracing ritual inoperativity means that one cannot set down one's tools before Sabbath begins and pick them up after the day is over without questioning how those tools are used and what system they reinforce. If the tools we use during "regular" life are stained with blood, our rituals

---

[59] Walter Benjamin, "Capitalism as Religion," in *Walter Benjamin: Selected Writings, Volume 1: 1913–1926,* ed. Marcus Bullock and Michael W. Jennings (Cambridge, MA: Belknap Press, 1996), 288.

do not represent real, messianic inoperativity, but rather the sovereignty of mechanization that forces us to look at others as soulless machines.

This paradox is at the heart of innumerable rituals outside of Sabbath, *shmita*, vigil, and fiesta, and if we had space here we could show how the same dynamic pervades all of them. Pope Francis articulates this paradox beautifully in a homily on fasting delivered for Lent, pointing out at first that fasting contradicts a "culture of 'doing,' of the 'useful,' where we exclude God from the horizon without realizing it. But we also exclude the horizon itself!"[60] What Pope Francis means is that fasting must be truly inoperative—it must do nothing. But then Francis goes on to insist that one must not "just fast" as if performing the ritual itself is the point. Instead, he argues that "fasting makes sense . . . if it leads to some benefit for others, if it helps us to cultivate the style of the Good Samaritan, who bends down to his brother in need and takes care of him." A casual listener of this homily might think Francis contradicts himself. If fasting is opposed to the absolute valorization of "doing" and "the useful," how can it be only valuable if it leads to "some benefit for others"? The answer is found in the paradox of inoperativity—fasting must be a ritual that creates a form of life characterized by giving to others. It is a ritual that must explode its own boundaries and affect our economic functioning, not merely in one corner of our lives, but in the totality of our existence.

This idea is the basis for everything that will follow in the rest of this book. In the next two chapters we do not talk much about rituals themselves. Instead, we talk about life within complex economies—and what inoperative rituals teach us life is supposed to be. Only in making dramatic ethical changes in

---

[60] Pope Francis, "Homily of Pope Francis: Basilica of Santa Sabina, Wednesday, March 5, 2014."

the way we look at the nonritual aspects of our lives can we genuinely arrive at an "ethics of doing nothing."

How does inoperativity change the way we look at life? The next chapter plots a course toward answering this question by focusing on perhaps the most obvious application: the ethics of work.

4

Doing Nothing and Work Ethics

If you were the GDP, your ideal citizen would be a compulsive gambler with cancer who's going through a drawn-out divorce that he copes with by popping fistfuls of Prozac and going berserk on Black Friday.

—Rutger Bregman, *Utopia for Realists*

"Doesn't Jeff Bezos have a right to be mad if you're clocked in for forty hours but only actually working for thirty? Aren't you stealing from him?"

—Job Training Instructor
at an Amazon Warehouse[1]

Peruse any pile of job applications or recommendation letters and you will find one intriguing term that emerges frequently alongside qualifiers such as *focused, team player,* and *tech savvy.* This term is, of course, *good work ethic.* It is fascinating partly because, in English, it always corresponds to one

---

[1] As quoted by Emily Guendelsberger, *On the Clock: What Low-Wage Work Did to Me, and How It Drives America Insane* (New York: Little, Brown and Company, 2019), 61.

simple thing: a willingness to do more work, with harder work. We rarely think of the term in conjunction to other significant questions about work or working culture.

Perhaps we should playfully broaden this term's meaning. If ethics is the realm contemplating human goods, we should think about how work can function as a human good, and how our other ethical commitments (perhaps drawn from our religious traditions) can inform the way we think about work. Furthermore, if rituals of inoperativity must paradoxically surpass their own boundaries so that they affect the entirety of life (as argued in the previous chapter), perhaps we should inquire how work relates to the ideal of an inoperative life. This chapter begins to offer an answer to this question.

Because the field of work is enormous, comprising domains as diverse as all human interests, the scope of this investigation is limited. The goal of this chapter is simply to reframe work, that is, to offer a different interpretation of its meaning, based on the central ideas developed in the previous three chapters. Naturally, such a reframing has multitudes of possible practical consequences, some of which will suggest themselves. But a total evaluation of the way the ethics of inoperativity affects work practices is far beyond the reach of what we can cover here. I focus instead on how the ethics of inoperative rituals shifts the existential value of work.

This chapter approaches this task in three steps. First, we examine a central principle derived from our exploration of inoperative rituals: that life transcends productive work. Second, following from this principle, we find that inoperative ethics challenges us to redefine how we understand the vice of sloth. Third, we discover that if sloth is not what we sometimes assume it is, this means that we must challenge the central feature of work in the modern world: status anxiety (and the different ways our economy reinforces and depends upon status anxiety). At the end of the chapter I show one possible application of these three steps, specifically an ethical endorsement of universal basic income.

Life Does Not Equal Work

When I teach general-education theology and ethics courses to undergraduates, I often show them what I call the "most difficult biblical command, and also the one your parents do not want you to follow." I refer to a mandate in Matthew 6:25, which may be translated bluntly, "Do not worry about your life." Most parents of college students desperately want them to worry about their lives, specifically by focusing on getting a degree that will provide them with high-paying work. Usually the students heartily concur with their parents and find themselves aggressively clamoring for the type of career that will define their lives positively.

The reason for the profound difficulty students (and all of us) face in following this command is that the modern world commonly (with some variation) equates life with work. Sometimes this equation is hidden and unconscious, and other times it may be explicit and self-aware. We find this equation latent in the terms we use for work, such as the phrase *making a living*. When young persons struggle to motivate themselves to find a good job, their parents might tell them, "Do something with your life." I remember overhearing a parent talking about her son's struggling career and saying, "He just cannot get his life going." We are schooled from a young age to assume that the generative aspect of life is work.

What does it mean to say that life equals work for many citizens of the modern world? A careful definition of terms is necessary here. By *work* I refer to material production (both as a worker or as a manager) or the creation of utilitarian services, as well as efforts to establish oneself as an effective worker.

Under this broad definition the term can also encompass behaviors that may not look like regular productive work. For example, work can include recreation and even practices that look like relaxation. This is the meaning behind the famous social theorist Thorstein Veblen's category of upper-class leisure. In order to avoid confusion, it is important to clarify that this term (in Veblen's analysis) has nothing to do with the way Pieper uses it, and the two uses of leisure are almost polar opposites. To explain why, I must offer a brief explanation of Veblen's argument, which is often misunderstood. His argument is also essential to showing why work has engulfed life in the modern world.

Veblen alleges that the difference between the lower and upper classes in societies is based around the division between two types of labor:

> The institution of a leisure class is the outgrowth of an early discrimination between employments, according to which some employments are worthy and others unworthy. Under this ancient distinction the worthy employments are those which may be classed as exploit; unworthy are those necessary everyday employments into which no appreciable element of exploit enters.[2]

By *exploit* Veblen refers to acts of predation, which in the ancient world included hunting and raiding, and in the modern world includes getting people to work for you or manipulating the environment or resources so that you can acquire an income passively (for example, profiting from rents or investments). The situation of the successful property magnate today is no different from that of the sinewy and cunning raider of barbarian times who has just forced a village into slavery—both use avaricious calculation to acquire a vast surplus of resources.

---

[2] Thorstein Veblen, *The Theory of the Leisure Class* (New York: Oxford University Press, 2007), 11.

What do you do when you are a dominant predator with a massive surplus? You can only use a tiny amount of it to meet your basic, alimentary necessities. The rest of it can only benefit you directly by enhancing your status. Consequently, according to Veblen, wealthy elites must expend enormous amounts of energy and capital on pointless rituals such as lavish weddings, vacations, soirees, fashion, and sports events because by doing so they can reveal the excess resources they possess and thus prove their status as effective predators. If they do not do this, they fail to demonstrate their status and risk losing their sense of dignity. Insofar as they wish to maintain their identities, they *must* engage in leisurely waste.

The point of Veblen's analysis is that much leisure we see in everyday life is not restful at all—it is not a truly pointless appreciation of created reality. Instead, it is hard, serious, self-oriented work, aimed at proving the value of one's life. This is why a rich person may truly feel exhausted after a day of casual shopping for sartorial amenities or planning an expensive wedding. Successful performance of these supposed leisurely activities is essential for establishing that one is a dominant member of the economic system, that one is truly "classy."

A person does not need to be a prominent member of the elite classes to engage in this type of work. All of us find ourselves regularly compelled to imitate whatever elements of elite-level leisure we can fit into our budgets (this is what Veblen called "invidious emulation"). Even the poorest family will often spend extravagantly to celebrate a wedding or visit an expensive restaurant, in order to feel—however remotely—that they share in the elite predatory status of those above them.

At this point let us do a brief calculation. If we combine the time we spend doing productive labor (in the usual sense of work for those of us who have regular jobs) and the time we spend imitating predatory elites through high-class leisure, we may comprehend in horror that the overwhelming majority of our lives are consumed with production-related industry or diligent attempts to elevate our status. We work to put food on our table and pay rent, and we work to pretend that we do not have to worry about buying food or paying rent. The dual elements of this all-encompassing phenomenon are what I call the work=life equation.

The end result of this equation is a worldview in which material production and management justify human existence. By *justify* I refer to both moral justification and epistemic justification (the ability to know what the human is)—partly because they are connected. Within the confines of the work=life equation, we view the entire category of value as either based on work or the demonstration of work status. Furthermore, as Pieper argued, the modern world since Kant has tended to view knowing as an act of productive work. As a consequence, productive work becomes the litmus test of what is real and valuable. This leads directly to a concept of human nature in which life, as well as the value we place on it, corresponds to the amount of active, productive labor performed.

Like many of the most deeply entrenched structures of civilization, the idea that life can be summed up by productive work is influential even without being explicitly stated. It is also compatible with the widespread recognition that other things in life are important besides work, such as vacations and time with family, because these phenomena quickly become absorbed into status symbols, which are merely significations of work.

In the third section of this chapter I provide a few technical reasons why we tend to equate life with work, and what (possibly) can be done to unsettle this equation. For now, I simply want to point out what is fundamentally wrong with this paradigm, per the ethical standpoint of inoperative rituals. A brief recapitulation of the arguments developed so far in this book demonstrate the crucial problem.

In Chapter 1 we found in religious rituals a model of human life fundamentally oriented toward inoperativity. Ritual behavior places humans in a state whereby the point of life is doing nothing, standing passively before the Absolute. If rituals represent our ultimate contact with "that which matters," we cannot accept that the meaning and justification of life can be found primarily in productive labor. If the philosophers of Chapter 1 were not convincing enough, the theologians of Chapter 2 were perhaps more so. Moltmann and Heschel showed us that the ultimate identity of God can be found in "doing nothing"—defined as pointless communion with creation, or the opposite of spatial covetousness. If God represents the goal of human identity—the *imago Dei*—and God exists through Sabbath, humans must find their ultimate *telos* in Sabbath as well. The paradox of inoperativity we explored in Chapter 3 demonstrates that the ritual element of inoperativity must affect not only sacral time for the worshipper but the worshipper's entire life framework, including politics and economics. Inoperative rituals can never be discrete. If they truly portray intrinsic goodness, life corresponds to "the good" to the extent that it mimics those rituals. Life cannot thus be measured by productive activity.

But what does this mean exactly? What is the point of saying that life does not equal work? We should not understand this statement in the popular, self-help sense that exhorts us to do other things than just working. The problem with this colloquial interpretation is that it often implies that time off for self-care is merely a means to help us work better or a means for us to establish Veblenian status symbols. Nor does the statement mean that we need more recreation, because as we have seen, recreation is simply another form of work, especially for status-seeking people.

Rather than being an injunction for more recreation, the denial that life=work means that human beings exist for something that supersedes material use, something that corresponds roughly to what has been called leisure, Sabbath, *shmita*, or fiesta. These practices are all linked to what Thomas Aquinas called the beatific vision. This term does not need to be cumbered with confessional theological baggage. We can understand the beatific vision as the logical implication of thinking about what productive work is for. When we have finished our work, when we have purchased our goods, when we have solved our material dilemmas—what is the purpose of all this? As Augustine said regarding the goodness of material things, "Take away the 'this' and 'that' and regard good itself if you can, then you will see God."[3] The goodness of God proceeds beyond material use, and this is why Heschel can describe God's being as Sabbath. For the same reason, the ultimate essence of human existence is Sabbath. If life is good, work does not equal life.

Perhaps this seems like a simple, obvious point. But when we examine it, we find that it can unsettle many of the commonplace assumptions about human identity and modern economics. The primary way in which this point affects the modern work ethic is by offering a different way to understand the age-old moral vice of sloth.

We Must Reframe Sloth

We all know that sloth is supposed to be evil. This is so in the majority of religious traditions and ethical frameworks. No one admires an indolent person. The Book of Proverbs is filled with admonitions against sloth, and perhaps the second-greatest insult one can use against a person in modern America is to call the person a "lazy bum" (the greatest insult, of course, is "fat," but in many minds the two epithets are closely related). Despite our tendency to unthinkingly disapprove of sloth, we should ask what makes sloth wrong. By giving an account of *how* sloth is evil (not merely that it is), we can demonstrate the dramatic effect of dismantling the work=life equation. As we

---

[3] Augustine, *De Trinitate,* 8:3. Augustine here is not talking about work but about things like food, health, and beauty. Nevertheless, his analysis also pertains to material work, because such work creates the things that we describe as good.

will see, sloth can be understood as evil in two different (and contradictory) ways. *How* we understand sloth to be wrong will deeply influence our work ethics.

As Christopher Jones and Conor Kelly observe, "The vice of sloth has a complicated history within Christian ethics and popular morality."[4] Jones and Kelly argue that there are two different religious explanations for what sloth is. In the American context, they argue that the universal disgust directed toward sloth arises from a specific kind of individualist ethos, best expressed by Max Weber's Protestant work ethic (although those who adopt this paradigm do not need to be Protestants). In this paradigm, sloth is evil because work demonstrates one's salvation. Originally, the Protestant immigrants to America understood salvation literally as redemption to paradise. Good, hard work was not the mechanism that led to salvation, but it was the clear and unmistakable sign that one had been saved. The obvious implication of this viewpoint is that "unwillingness to work is symptomatic of the lack of grace," as Weber put it.[5]

Weber's historical link between Protestant thinking and capitalism has been roundly debated.[6] Still, one aspect of his argument is certain: The basic idea of work as an expression of one's status as "saved" is indubitably rife in American culture. This idea persists in a secularized form even among Americans who lack the Protestant or general Christian beliefs associated with it. Salvation, for the vaguely or nonreligious American today, consists in self-actualization, or the ability to enjoy the pleasures of life independently without relying on a helping

[4] Christopher D. Jones and Conor M. Kelly, "Sloth: America's Ironic Structural Vice," *Journal of the Society of Christian Ethics* 37, no. 2 (Fall 2017): 122.

[5] Max Weber, *The Protestant Ethic and the Spirit of Capitalism,* trans. Talcott Parsons (New York: Charles Scribner's Sons, 1958), 159.

[6] For a summary of criticisms and defenses of Weber's historical thesis, see Max L. Stackhouse, "Weber, Theology, and Economics," in *The Oxford Handbook of Christianity and Economics,* ed. Paul Oslington (New York: Oxford University Press, 2014), 307–36.

hand from anyone else.[7] In this mindset, secularized "grace" corresponds to luck, or the endowments of superior genetics or social breeding. The "righteous life" of the average American thus consists in a series of secularized theological concepts. The first is predestination, which includes being born with a symmetrical face, clear skin, an athletic build, a higher-than-average IQ, and wealthy parents who will pay for robust private education and extracurricular activities. The second theological element in the sequence is justification, in which one recognizes these predestined endowments and decides to accept them and use them to their maximal purpose. What follows is sanctification—the rigorous, never-ending process whereby grace reveals itself in good works—high-level educational attainment, prowess in sports, business prosperity, and finally retirement in wealth and fame (glorification). The common thread in this sequence of soteriological phenomena is work—the glory of the ultimate human is the perfection of work attainments.

What is sloth in this paradigm? It is a failure fully to define oneself by one's work or to work maximally. The slothful person—in the standard modern American mindset—rejects grace by refusing to build up the self through material output. Lazy people, who do not work to their fullest potential, are evil because they are incomplete—they have de facto aborted themselves. We look at such persons with a mixture of fear, loathing, and pity, because we perceive them as subhuman—having dehumanized themselves by their inability or unwillingness to truly live as we understand life. If life equals work, the person who works insufficiently is less than completely alive.

---

[7] Numerous thinkers have pointed out that many modern economic mindsets are tacitly religious in several ways, including in the brief format I suggest here. See, for example, Robert H. Nelson's two volumes, *Reaching for Heaven on Earth: The Theological Meaning of Economics* (Lanham, MD: Rowman and Littlefield, 1991), and *Economics as Religion: From Samuelson to Chicago and Beyond* (University Park: Pennsylvania State University Press, 2001).

When we see homeless persons sitting under a bridge in squalor drinking beer, we feel an uncanny emotion that they should not exist—they should either get a job or die. The more compassionate among us hope for the former, the less compassionate the latter. Most of us are emotionally somewhere in between.

This explanation of the evil of sloth makes intuitive sense to many of us. But there is another account of sloth available in Christian tradition. Jones and Kelly point back to Thomas Aquinas as the best representative of this alternative portrait: "For Aquinas, sloth is a sin against charity, the chief theological virtue."[8] Charity, in Aquinas and numerous other Christian theologians, is the phenomenon in which human beings encounter God, for "God is love" (Jn 4:8). As a virtue, it displays itself in compassionate friendships toward other human beings and a resulting willingness to work not simply for the sake of work, but for the common good. Jones and Kelly also observe that one of the chief qualities of charity is a joyful attitude toward life, which is not identical to simply "being in a good mood," but is rather a fervent belief in the goodness of all created reality, for charity requires "a habit of rejoicing in the presence of what one loves."[9] Charity thus depends upon a mode of perception, an ability to recognize inherent goodness within the world. For that reason it corresponds closely with Pieper's understanding of leisure. This is why, as we found in Chapter 2, Pieper claims that acedia or sloth is part of the antithesis of leisure, as much so as overwork. Both greedy workaholism and sloth fail to rejoice in creation and therefore are sins against charity.

In this second paradigm a slothful person sins by not perceiving and embracing present reality. Such a person has no passion for the well-being of others and therefore does not contribute to the interwoven thread of collective human existence. In this sense sloth is an antisocial sin. But at a simpler

[8] Jones and Kelly, "Sloth," 123.
[9] Jones and Kelly, 123.

level, sloth is a failure of contemplation. The slothful person has no desire to see God in the faces of others and therefore to be obligated to loving service. Hence, sloth causes us to seek out distractions that will prevent us from recognizing suffering and our responsibilities to alleviate it. Sloth urges us to occupy our minds with trivial matters so that we do not think about who we truly are. Paradoxically, sloth can make us very busy.

This second explanation of sloth is similar to the first one described above in one way: It portrays sloth as a failure to embrace life. The key difference is that in the standard American account of sloth, the point is that life is work. Thus, we admire anyone who "hustles" hard and works diligently, regardless of what the purpose of this work is. We celebrate space missions and billionaires who design rockets potentially to colonize Mars, simply because we think "doing hard things" is a good in itself. The end result is that we glamorize the equivalent of playing with large, expensive toys. We admire athletes who play games if they work hard at training and playing those games. Here I do not intend to judge the character of billionaire inventors or professional athletes; I only wish to point out that the outsized attention and respect these domains of human endeavor receive reflect our valorization of work as the summation of life.

The Thomist account of sloth, on the other hand, identifies life with charity. The hardworking person avoids the sin of sloth in this framework only to the extent that such a person works in order joyfully to be present with others. Hence this approach requires a refusal to judge whether people are slothful merely on the basis of how much productive work they do. When we look at homeless people living under a bridge, we cannot say whether they strive in their relationships to apply charity toward others any more than do those who have houses or apartments and regular jobs. Furthermore, we would be appalling hypocrites for claiming that they are uncharitable, given that such a judgment would itself be a sign of uncharity.

The Thomistic identification of sloth with lack of charity also implies that sloth may reveal itself in doing too much work, if such work stands against charity. There are cases in which doing nothing is more anti-slothful than working hard. While I was studying for ministry at seminary, I remember a professor proclaim the existence of the "noble F," which he claimed occurs when a student with family obligations consciously chooses to set an assignment aside in order to be present with family and thus gets a lower grade than might have been possible. The fact that such noble F's are not recognized and celebrated in other areas of human life shows one of the central ways in which we conflate life with productive material work, and thus do not recognize the value of parental childcare and elderly parent care. We find this sentiment visible when someone says of a particular parent (usually a woman) that "she does not work; she stays home and cares for the kids." When you combine this sentiment with the tendency for some married heterosexual women to blend their identity with their husband's (the classic Mrs. John Smith), a frightening possibility emerges: Perhaps we do not fully believe that nonmarket-based caregivers are fully alive. A mindset that equates life with work will frame them as slothful appendages to the working people who "support" them. Recently, some economists and ethicists have pushed for recognizing nonmarket-based caregivers as legitimate workers—and while I applaud this approach for many reasons, I wonder if we ought to question the underlying assumption: that work is synonymous with value in life, and that therefore only working people are valuable. If fully significant life does not equal work, whether a person "works" caring for dependents or "works" in an office or job site is irrelevant to a person's moral status or claim to life. Such persons are only guilty of sloth if they neglect concern for the community within which they play a role, no matter how that role looks.

The point of the above observations regarding sloth is simple: If we delink life and work, our attitude toward work itself must change. Our fear of sloth must cease causing us to valorize work in an absolute sense. As work grows less central in our estimation of the value of other humans, several other work-related attitudes will shift. We will become more capable of confronting the prejudices we display toward the elderly, the poor, the homeless, the disabled, and numerous other groups. We will also perceive economic data differently. Rather than grading the economy on the basis of unemployment statistics, we will ask how current job numbers reflect improved access to life among citizens. Do increases in employment or GDP truly reflect increasing abilities on the part of citizens to appreciate the goodness of world?

Reframing sloth will also enable us to address one of the most horrendous, cancerous outcomes of a *homo faber* anthropology: work-induced status anxiety.

We Must Challenge Work-Induced Status Anxiety

Status anxiety is pervasive in many cultures, even though its foggy nature makes it difficult to measure with precise statistics. Recalling Alain de Botton's historical overview mentioned in the Introduction, we may define status anxiety as a sharp, excruciating feeling that one has not lived up to one's full potential, or that one has no real potential at all. It may display itself in sundry ways—depression, midlife crisis, a feeling of irrelevance, or as a general sense that one's existence is constantly under question.

Ellen Ruppel Shell situates the roots of status anxiety in America in the mid-1800s in a type of mythology promoted by preachers such as Horatio Alger, who fetishized the idea of "the self-made man" who could rise from destitution to wealth simply by cunning and hard work. Alger's *Street Life in New York with the Boot Blacks* was a popular example of literature promoting this idea, and Shell adds that "Alger, a defrocked minister, published nearly one hundred novels built around this theme, a message given credence by wealthy industrialists of the time whose fondest boast was of being 'self-made.'"[10] Believing that it is always possible to overcome all odds and achieve success through work is a tantalizing concept, and one that many Americans and Europeans find thrilling and even morally requisite. During lectures in my ethics classes I sometimes ask my students if they believe that it is always possible to do anything you put your mind to. I routinely find that many of my students not only believe this slogan, but hold it as an article of faith that must not be questioned. To their great shock and dismay, I then point out that this belief is manifestly falsifiable. For example, I tell them, as an adult in my early thirties who has never played a sport beyond the most rudimentary level, it would be absurd for me to think that I could—with enough effort—play in the NBA. To me, this fact seems stunningly obvious. Nevertheless, although I do persuade some students with this example, many argue against it anyway.

My students' insistence on the infinite potential of hard work is a key element of the status-anxiety culture, fueled by the idea that work=life. When work becomes the summation of all value, it attains godlike status, which implies omnipotence. Suggesting there are limitations on what work can do is thus blasphemy. Blind faith in the justifying grace of work leads to subsequent cognitive errors, like overestimating the occurrence of uncommon things. We cannot allow ourselves to recognize that most people who are born poor stay poor and that most of the rich are born rich, and thus we latch on to stories of how "I started at the bottom, and now I'm here." According to research by the Pew Charitable Trusts, the odds of climbing to the upper-middle class (the top 20 percent of earners) in America for those born into poverty are somewhere in the

<hr/>

[10] Ellen Ruppel Shell, *The Job: Work and Its Future in a Time of Radical Change* (New York: Currency, 2018), 55.

single digits.[11] Even the odds of making it into the middle class are quite steep.[12] Nevertheless, some people make it, and these people constitute the righteous "saints" we must emulate. The upshot is that unusual situations become normative, and people have no excuses for their lot in life.

The fist-pumping phrase "no excuses" is another quintessentially American utterance, proclaimed in gym soliloquies and employee pep talks *ad nauseam*. It has a particularly egregious outcome: a crushing burden of shame. This shame is a central function of status anxiety. Without excuses, workers find themselves in a chronic condition of personal culpability. The infinitely high standard set by the vision of the American dream leaves them with a nagging sense that they could always do more to justify their existence. Committed to avoiding the slothful fatalism of someone who gives up, workers may continually strive for an elusive goal of success that never materializes. Life thereby becomes a vicious cycle of status anxiety leading to hard work, followed by an awareness of competitive deficiency (with "no excuses" for the ensuing guilt), which then leads to greater status anxiety, and so on. Opportunities for economic penance do not exist. The only conceivable "off ramps" are mental collapse or suicide, the latter increasingly chosen by workers in times of economic crisis.[13]

---

[11] See Pew Charitable Trust, "Moving on Up: Why Do Some Americans Leave the Bottom of the Economic Ladder, But Not Others?" (November 2013). The researchers claimed that about 4 percent of persons born into the bottom quintile of family income made it into the top quintile.

[12] See Pew Charitable Trust. Researchers found that around 30 percent of those in the bottom quintile made it into the middle class.

[13] The data showing the commonsense correlation between unemployment or financial instability and suicide is (unsurprisingly) clear. See, for example, Nikolaos Antonakakis and Alan Collins, "The Impact of Fiscal Austerity on Suicide: On the Empirics of a Modern Greek Tragedy," *Social Science and Medicine* 112 (July 2014). Antonakakis and Collins focus on the situation in Greece, but the same situation has been observed elsewhere. See, for example, Tetsuya Matsubayashi, Kozue Sekijima, and Michiko Ueda, "Government

There are reasons to believe that recent developments in modern economies have not only supported this twisted labyrinth of status anxiety but have directly constructed it. Perhaps the most prominent mechanism for enforcing status anxiety initially appears welcoming and liberative, thus masking its dystopian implications. I refer to the idealization of "worker flexibility."

Economists have documented that over the latter half of the twentieth century and through the first part of the twenty-first, employers ceased offering job stability as a chief lure for new hires and replaced it with offers of flexibility.[14] A cunning euphemism, flexibility points to a situation in which temporary workers may find great jobs, but these jobs can disappear overnight, and the schedules, pay, and benefits they offer may vary wildly. Nick Srnicek and Alex Williams observe that compared to the jobs common in the previous century, "today's jobs typically involve more casual working hours, low and stagnant wages, decreasing job protections, and widespread insecurity."[15] Numerous low-wage jobs in fields as diverse as law enforcement, sales, and even college-level instruction are qualified as part time, which seems to imply that they are jobs held by persons who do not need to work full time, but that is rarely true. Most workers in these fields juggle several part-time jobs at once, or maintain only one of them and then supplement their income with sporadic side jobs. For example, a religion professor colleague of mine teaches during the semester and works at an Amazon warehouse during breaks. I myself have

---

Spending, Recession, and Suicide: Evidence from Japan," *BMC Public Health* 20, no. 243 (2020).

[14] See Shell, *The Job,* 60–61. For an early study that recognized this ongoing trend, see Henry S. Farber, "Are Lifetime Jobs Disappearing? Job Duration in the United States, 1973–1993," in *Labor Statistics Measurement Issues,* ed. John Haltiwanger, Marilyn E. Manser, and Robert Topel (Chicago: University of Chicago Press, 1998), 157–206.

[15] Nick Srnicek and Alex Williams, *Inventing the Future: Postcapitalism and a World without Work* (London: Verso, 2016), 93.

sometimes supplemented my fluctuating academic income with odd jobs in construction and other areas. Shell quotes a personal interview with economist Guy Standing, who points out that we have "idealized the idea of portable work, promoting the notion of people roaming about with a portfolio of skills at a price they set themselves." This ideal seems pleasant because of the theoretical freedom associated with such a lifestyle, but Standing notices its frightening implication: "The person who works for himself works for a tyrant—you are only as good as your last job and your last performance."[16] Such a tyranny of the self has direct implications for affirming the life=work equation and resulting status anxiety.

Sociologist Allison Pugh has documented the various ways pervasive work instability influences our perception of ourselves and the continuity of our lives in what she calls "the tumbleweed society."[17] One of these implications is that in the gig economy we are continually forced to think of our lives as defined by work. If we must promote ourselves for a new job every few months, or constantly reapply for new projects within an organization, our identity as a worker becomes central to every preoccupation of our mind. Business-management researchers Sally Maitlis and Scott Sonenshein argue that this can lead to a "crisis of sensemaking" in which a worker's identity is constantly shifting with each new role undertaken, leading to cognitive disruption.[18] Minor emotional stress associated with new work can be positive—it can fuel creativity and fight boredom. But in excess, and when workers lack control over the circumstances, it creates scenarios in which workers must continually rework themselves because of how transient each

---

[16] Quoted in Shell, *The Job,* 61.

[17] See Allison J. Pugh, *The Tumbleweed Society: Working and Caring in an Age of Insecurity* (New York: Oxford University Press, 2015).

[18] See Sally Maitlis and Scott Sonenshein, "Sensemaking in Crisis and Change: Inspirations and Insight from Weick (1988)," *Journal of Management Studies* 47, no. 3 (May 2010): 551–74.

job may be. Being required to craft a resume and cover letter too frequently creates a mindset in which work comprises the defining features of one's existence, and the boss's "yes" or "no" balloons from a minor hiccup in life to a cataclysmic ontological signifier. In short, such a work situation directly prevents anyone from following the command of Matthew 6:25: "Do not worry about your life." By making work chronically unstable, the modern economy forces us to make work the core proposition regarding our identity and simultaneously forces us to worry about it.

Guy Standing argues that twenty-first-century markets have thus created a new and expanding social class, which he calls the "precariat."[19] This class is unique in that it is not strictly poor, in the straightforward sense of being low income. Large numbers of this class are poor, but they may also be well within the middle class (though they frequently pop in and out of classes depending on their current employment). Standing's term is obviously a portmanteau of *precarious* and *proletariat,* and this combination hints at the main idea that this class works like the proletariat, but with "minimal trust relationships with capital or the state."[20] The relationship of those in the precariat to their employers and beneficiaries in government is strictly a relationship of *performance.* No feature of their life bears value to the world except their work contributions. Contrasting the precariat with a class he calls the *salariat* (another obvious portmanteau), Standing points out that the precariat are "in career-less jobs, without traditions of social memory, a feeling that they belong in an occupational community steeped in stable practices, codes of ethics and norms of behaviour, reciprocity and fraternity."[21] As a member of the precariat, if you work well, you matter; if not, you disappear.

---

[19] See Guy Standing, *The Precariat: The New Dangerous Class* (London: Bloomsbury Academic, 2021).

[20] Standing, 9.

[21] Standing, 14.

At one level there is nothing unethical about precariousness, if it is freely chosen. For example, consider a daredevil who wishes to dangle at the edge of a cliff for an adrenaline rush. We may question the prudence of stunts like this, but few would argue that such behavior should be banned in all circumstances. This type of consensual, volition-based precariousness corresponds with what Standing designates as a "romanticized" vision of the economic precariat—individuals who like to be free and nomadic, traveling regularly and working at different jobs, often during their youth. However, we might ponder the ethical implications of *forcing* someone to dangle at the edge of a cliff. Imagine that as I stroll along an outcropping of the Grand Canyon and observe a rock climber casually flopping her legs over the chasm, I were to decide to grab a stranger and force him to mimic this action. Clearly, this would constitute a traumatizing form of assault. Why? To put it mildly—and leaving aside the violation of bodily integrity in using physical force—I would be coercing this individual to excessively "worry about his life." Forced precariousness—unlike the whimsical liberty of daredevils—brings acute, severe trauma by placing the overwhelming weight of one's existence into one's capacity to do something—to work.

One might wonder why the current Western economy insists on maintaining this precariat class. We need no elaborate conspiracy theories to answer this question. As Standing, Pugh, Shell, and other thinkers explain, forced precariousness increases production and efficiency at a massive scale in the current business environment. In a constantly evolving tech economy, where innovations and shifts of capital create and remove job opportunities seemingly overnight, the best strategy for building an effective enterprise is to make human labor as elastic as possible—which means being able to toss aside workers like used plastic plates. No one worker needs to be doing anything for too long. In addition to the efficiency created by this perpetual flux, Kathryn Tanner argues that the fear induced by constant job insecurity creates workers who are effortlessly malleable and can be easily controlled by managers.[22] A worker who has been fired, relocated, and retrained enough times will eventually become a compliant zombie, craving stability at any cost. Employee pushback in the form of unionizing or general foot-dragging becomes less of a problem for managers as a result of the constant shifting of labor.

Shell describes a prominent example of this rapidly evolving labor scene in the drone industry. Business forecasters had predicted at the beginning of the 2010s that the American economy would require a multitude of well-trained drone operators within a few years. It turned out that this prediction was right; drone technology became a lucrative rage in the mid-2010s. Universities and community colleges trained scores of young engineers to operate drones for surveying, photography, law enforcement, and numerous other purposes.

However, just as soon as the drone boom echoed into the tech world, it suddenly went silent. Thousands of licensed drone operators flooded the market. Analysts had glowingly prophesied that mastering new drone technology would give workers a golden ticket to a well-paid, stable job, but the gilding on this ticket quickly succumbed to corrosive inflation. By the end of 2017, Shell observes, "the average salary for drone pilots had leveled out at roughly $30,000."[23] Drone engineers who had spent years and dollars gaining expertise in a new domain of technological prowess suddenly discovered that their effort could only earn them the standard of living of someone

---

[22] Kathryn Tanner, *Christianity and the New Spirit of Capitalism* (New Haven, CT: Yale University Press, 2019), 65. Tanner argues that the presence of low-paid and temporary workers in workplaces functions as a constant reminder of an "implied threat"—no worker is irreplaceable.

[23] Shell, *The Job,* 188.

who had stayed in an old-fashioned discipline like substitute teaching.

Part of the reason why the drone boom failed to provide long-term, high-level employment is that drones got better—easier to program and use. Shell searched for a reason why formerly giddy drone operators were facing failed job prospects and got a simple answer: "There are a lot of people who know how to fly drones."[24] This example is not isolated. Pugh observes that in Silicon Valley tech companies, it is common for half the workforce to be replaced every year.[25] We might assume that technology employees are already upper class and that therefore they can handle the instability, and that is generally true.[26] However, flexible employment is by no means only a feature of the elite economy. As Matthew Desmond has shown, unstable work gets even worse for people in poorer, low-skilled work environments.[27] Once the rapid-fire economy finds enough workers to sate its erratic appetite, it spits them out into the market place, where they must scramble to "re-flavor" themselves for the next temporary employment binge.

The precariat, flexible employment, and treating people like used plastic plates—such cruel features of our modern world create a vicious circle in which we feel chronic instability and try to address it by progressively identifying ourselves more with our work. Like a helpless animal being tossed in the air,

---

[24] Shell, 189.

[25] See Pugh, *The Tumbleweed Society*, 6.

[26] Pugh reports that a few generally secure upper-class workers find employment instability to be exciting—and the thrills associated with constant novelty might be the root cause of our romanticizing of "flexible employment" (see Pugh, 9–10). Of course, the experiences of rich persons who have the freedom to change jobs whenever they wish cannot be taken as replicative of the experiences of poorer persons for whom the loss of a job may mean homelessness or worse.

[27] See Matthew Desmond, "Disposable Ties and the Urban Poor," *American Journal of Sociology* 117, no. 5 (2012): 1295–1335.

we grasp randomly at whatever might give us a sense of safety, and the thing we grab most often is the very thing throwing us around—our work. This tragic reality is a central part of what Pope Francis has called the "throwaway culture." In his encyclical *Fratelli Tutti,* Francis highlights the "obsession with reducing labour costs with no concern for its grave consequences" as a central aspect of a culture that views human beings as expendable objects (no. 20). As despicable as this attitude may be, it is crucial to observe that it does not arise from outright malevolence on the part of employers. Nobody wants to throw anyone away or make life precarious. The frightening impetus for these things is a *homo faber* anthropology, in which a person's life is defined by work. Such a view of humanity makes humans valuable as long as they provide productive work and instantly dehumanizes them when they can no longer do so. This makes status anxiety not merely incidental to life in the modern world but constitutive of it. *If you are not worrying about your life, you are not human.* This means that superficial fixes to our anxiety problem, such as more psycho-therapeutic drugs, company retreats, vacation time, or comfy couches in workspaces—while perhaps laudable in themselves—cannot solve our problem. An ethic of inoperativity calls us to directly question the life=work matrix that is reinforced by precarious employment, and to reframe employment as something a person does to facilitate a life well lived rather than the essence of that life itself.

The ethics of inoperative rituals thus calls us to make practical and political changes in our economic structures. A thorough analysis of Sabbath-keeping, vigil observance, and fiesta propels us to an economic mandate to reform the way society orchestrates our work, so as to confront and combat the life=work equation that has intertwined itself into the fabric of our consciousness. This leads us to the final point of this chapter.

Application:
We Must Build an Economy Aimed at Inoperativity

If rituals teach us that the point of life is to observe the good-ness around us in charitable communion with others, we must consider how we can structure our economic systems to that end. We must not be blind to the difficulty of this task.

Our current work culture leverages a host of mechanisms that shroud our consciousness with the illusion that work is life, thus compelling us to avoid sloth by increasing status anxiety. The vogue societal and familial pressure to succeed through long working hours and relentless competitiveness is an obvious mechanism of this system. But some of the most influential work=life mechanisms are subliminal or even barely noticeable from an insider's perspective. For example, Michael Fischer and Sally Applin's research into work culture has highlighted the role of surveillance technology on mak-ing employees feel increased identification with their work, particularly because of how surveillance promotes a sense of being constantly under question in one's work.[28] Employers such as restaurants, bars, factories, and even large-scale insti-tutions like the Transportation Security Administration (TSA) have installed innumerable cameras that give employees a sense of relentless observation. Fischer and Applin argue that while working in this state, employees are induced to think of themselves as melded with the job, thus losing their mental agency. Because the surveillance erodes (or at least qualifies) the modicum of trust that exists between workers and bosses, workers must confront a chronic maxim to prove themselves by being busy. While on the job, work and existence thereby

---

[28] See Sally A. Applin and Michael D. Fischer, "Watching Me, Watching You: Process Surveillance and Agency in the Workplace," 2013 IEEE Inter-national Symposium on Technology and Society (ISTAS): Social Implications of Wearable Computing and Augmediated Reality in Everyday Life (2013): 268–75.

become indistinguishable. Shell writes that "the constant sur-veillance of employees diminishes their capacity to operate as independent thinkers and actors."[29]

There is no easy way to directly alter these subtle mecha-nisms of the work=life equation. Also, because of the scope of this book, there is no space to address all of them. Hence, rather than offering a laundry list of controversial policies, I suggest one—universal basic income (UBI)—that could be vital for breaking the adamantine linkage between work and life in the modern economy. I have chosen to suggest this measure for two reasons: (1) It is relatively nonpartisan, and key thinkers from many political camps have defended it; and (2) the pri-mary reason many people oppose it boils down to a firm faith in a *homo faber* anthropology, which it is the intention of this book to undermine. I do not offer a wholesale endorsement of this policy—a plethora of technical questions need to be an-swered first. Instead of an absolute endorsement, what follows is an ethical analysis of this policy that will reveal it to be an example of the type of new economic thinking that we must attempt if we wish to upend the work=life equation and move toward a society-wide consensus that life is charity.

Universal Basic Income

As many economists, social theorists, and pundits have em-phasized, UBI is not a new idea. Prominent intellectual heroes ranging from Thomas Paine to Martin Luther King Jr. have promoted it, though they are not widely known for doing so.[30] One of the most surprising early advocates for something like modern UBI theories was the libertarian economist Milton

---

[29] Shell, *The Job,* 128.

[30] For an overview of the history of UBI, see Juliana Uhuru Bidadanure, "The Political Theory of Universal Basic Income," *Annual Review of Political Science* 22, no. 1 (May 2019): 481–501.

Friedman, who called his theory a "negative income tax."[31] Although the idea as he expressed it was never adopted, it became a crucial influence on the development of the Earned Income Tax Credit—a central (and widely applauded) feature of the US tax system.[32] The gist of UBI is simple: a tax cull should deliver "payments to all citizens for—well—being alive."[33] It sounds like a wildly leftwing policy (and most of its proponents do come from the left), but it often receives robust defenses from libertarian thinkers. In addition to Milton Friedman, UBI has also been defended by Friedrich Hayek (though not in an explicit form), and more recently by conservative/libertarian economist Charles Murray.[34] Conservative and libertarian thinkers admire it primarily for its simplicity and potential to obviate the blundering bureaucratic welfare state. By providing a low-yet-wide social safety net, UBI promises to be the last reaching grasp across the finish line of ending poverty, at least in nation-states that have wealth enough to enact it.

Whether UBI in its current stages is a realistic policy for immediate application is not a question I can answer here. This is not because UBI lacks scientific evidence in its favor. As Rutger Bregman has argued, almost all UBI experiments conducted over the last century in places as diverse as Canada and India have been stellar successes, demonstrating that giving people free money does not cause massive unemployment,

---

[31] See Milton Friedman, *Capitalism and Freedom* (Chicago: University of Chicago Press, 1962), 182–89.

[32] Friedman's influence on the development of the Earned Income Tax Credit is explained in an interview with Stanford historian Jennifer Burns. See Clifton B. Parker, "Stanford Scholar Explores Pros, Cons of 'Basic Income,'" *Stanford News*, August 8, 2018.

[33] Shell, *The Job,* 315.

[34] See Friedrich Hayek, *The Road to Serfdom* (Chicago: University of Chicago Press, 1944), 147–48; Charles Murray, "A Guaranteed Income for Every American," *Wall Street Journal,* June 3, 2016.

inflation, or declines in productivity.[35] The reason my comments will be general is that UBI has never been tested on a truly large scale, and critics are quick to point out that this is an ambiguity that raises dangers. Rather than engage in speculative number crunching. I will focus on UBI's ethical justification. What I can argue without hesitation is that the basic principle behind UBI is one that follows from the ethics of inoperativity I have charted in this book thus far. This principle is that work and life must be disentangled in our future economic systems.

The key word to apply in any ethical evaluation of UBI is *future.* Part of the reason why UBI makes sense as an ethical proposition is that, in broad terms, our planet is becoming immensely rich. What *rich* means here needs to be qualified, both in terms of content and relativity. Barring a Malthusian problem of massive overpopulation, or a global catastrophe reducing population by a large margin, it is probable that we can create a world in which the amount of work needed to provide the basic necessities of life (food, shelter, water, security, healthcare, and clothing—what I refer to as alimentary resources) gradually decreases to miniscule levels per capita. This is not a controversial idea, and almost everyone knows it abstractly, though our unconscious fears of either a Malthusian problem or a global mass-mortality scenario keep us from thinking about it too much. At the time of writing, in Europe, Australia, and much of Asia and North and South America, it is easy to envision a scenario of basic alimentary sufficiency, with either a small working population or short working hours

---

[35] See Rutger Bregman, *Utopia for Realists: How We Can Build the Ideal World,* trans. Elizabeth Manton (New York: Little, Brown and Company, 2017), 25–50. Bregman mounts convincing evidence that when given no-strings-attached money, poor people behave more rationally than they would in a state of poverty, and that UBI systems could actually save money in the long term.

(or a combination of both).[36] As Steven Pinker's analysis has shown, the main driver for this increasing efficiency in alimentary resources is technology.[37] Technology cannot perform several types of hard work, but it can speed up the process of long work (for example, planes replacing covered wagons), or simply take care of it while human operators do other things (for example, washing machines). Technology in the form of agricultural improvements also makes land far more efficient at feeding populations.

Because I wish to avoid even the most tentative predictions about the future, I will not dare to estimate how much work will be necessary for alimentary sufficiency by the middle or the end of the present century. In lieu of arbitrary estimates, then, allow me to present a purely hypothetical scenario. Imagine a world in which only 20 percent of human biological effort and time are needed to maintain sufficient food, water, shelter, clothing, security, and healthcare for everyone. Such a world is realistic—some might argue we are already in such a world—and I have deliberately chosen a number higher than the most astute futurists use. In the 1960s, experts at the RAND Corporation predicted that soon only 2 percent of the population would be engaged in alimentary work.[38] The slow, steady pace of automation is year by year making alimentary work more ef-

---

[36] It is important to emphasize that many parts of the world, especially Southeast Asia and much of Africa, are not even close to alimentary sufficiency at present. However, this is not the result of deficiencies in resources—these parts of the world are some of the most lush in natural goods (consider, for example, the Democratic Republic of the Congo). The causes are political: the results of foreign exploitation, corrupt governments, ongoing military conflicts, and lack of access to education.

[37] Chapters 6–8 of Steven Pinker, *Enlightenment Now: The Case for Reason, Science, Humanism, and Progress* (New York: Viking, 2018), document the mammoth increases in technological efficiency accomplished by the end of the twentieth century. For a similar analysis, see Gregg Easterbrook, *It's Better Than It Looks: Reasons for Optimism in an Age of Fear* (New York: Public Affairs, 2018), 1–22.

[38] See Bregman, *Utopia for Realists,* 132.

ficient. A study from the McKinsey Global Institute found that
64 percent of manufacturing work in forty-six countries could
be fully automated with the robotic technology available in
2017.[39] Along the same lines, Srnicek and Williams point to
sober statistical estimations indicating that 47 to 80 percent of
jobs in the mid-2010s were fully automatable.[40] Whether and
how much these numbers will increase is unknown, but it takes
herculean mental effort to think they will not. Be that as it may,
my only requirement for the current thought experiment is to
imagine that this number *could* increase to 80 percent across
all alimentary forms of work. What would most of us be doing
with ourselves in such a world?

Under the current hegemony of the life=work equation, the
answer is simple: We would still be forced to work to "make a
living," though not at alimentary automatable tasks. The small
percentage of expert workers needed for maintaining the machines and managing societal functioning would be robustly
busy, perhaps, but the rest of us would occupy ourselves with
other things. For example, the media entertainment industry
might thrive in such a world. Bartending, dancing, and sex work
might remain as well. Mental-health therapists would be fairly
important in this world, perhaps more so than now, as Isaac
Asimov predicted in 1964 regarding his vision of what 2014
would look like.[41] However, due to the law of supply and demand, the competition for jobs in these domains would increase.
Also, because jobs in fields such as entertainment and recreation

---

[39] See Michael Chui, Katy George, James Manyika, and Mehdi Miradi,
"Human+Machine: A New Era of Automation in Manufacturing," *McKinsey
Insights* (September 7, 2017).

[40] See Srnicek and Williams, *Inventing the Future,* 112.

[41] Asimov wrote that "mankind will suffer badly from the disease of bore-
dom, a disease spreading more widely each year and growing in intensity.
This will have serious mental, emotional and sociological consequences, and
I dare say that psychiatry will be far and away the most important medical
specialty in 2014." See Isaac Asimov, "Visit to the World's Fair of 2014,"
New York Times, August 16, 1964.

are notoriously fickle, the precariat class would rapidly expand in such an economy. Most workers would spend gargantuan shares of time looking for new jobs or retooling themselves for different types of work. The weight of status anxiety could be crushing.

What alternatives do we have? Obviously we would need to choose between UBI and some kind of work-based supplemental income strategy. Practical problems with the latter option abound. If we continued to use work as the primary criterion for deciding who deserves what, when work is not as necessary as it once was, those who own the means to work (whether federal bureaucrats or private corporations) would gain unprecedented power to manipulate human behavior. Such entities might not only force us to work in uncomfortable roles, they might also draft us into vanity projects ("pyramid building"). The reason for this impulse emerges from what economists call Say's Law—that production creates its own demand.[42] Many economists believe this principle to be partially wrong, because humans do not have an infinite desire for unnecessary goods.[43] Nevertheless, to some extent, especially in technological industry and fashion, the principle does hold true—most of us want things that we do not truly need. Veblen's analysis explains why we buy these things—we want to emulate predatory prowess, to reach for higher status. We want to demonstrate our working ability. The result is that economic powerbrokers potentially have infinite power to make human beings do unnecessary things, simply because they can. If a capitalist can convince the upper classes that they need a large number of pointless widgets in order to look powerful, fairly soon everyone will need such widgets, and if people must work to live, they will be de facto dragooned into making widgets.

---

[42] See Jean Baptiste Say, *A Treatise on Political Economy,* trans. Charles Prinsepp and Clement Biddle (Philadelphia: Grigg and Eliott, 1845), 138–39.

[43] This was the fundamental basis for Keynes's objection to Say's law. See John Maynard Keynes, *General Theory of Employment, Interest, and Money,* vol. 1 (New York: Routledge, 1997), 215.

The result of this type of work scenario would possibly be even worse than what Marx called "alienation," because in alimentary industry at least the workers may conceive of themselves as improving the world for everyone in some way. A world where work is not necessary for alimentary security but still mandated by economic powers would be one in which swathes of the population could be turned into legions of virtual gladiators, competing for life-supporting jobs for the pleasure of those above them, or prostitutes (sexual or nonsexual) forced to provide work-based pleasure under the threat of economic pain.

One could reasonably argue that this is what a large sector of the current "developed" economy has already become. Anthropologist David Graeber provides an enormous amount of research suggesting that possibly more than 50 percent of jobs in the United States in the 2010s were "bullshit jobs," meaning that they were jobs that contribute very little (or even nothing) intrinsically valuable to the economy, and are sometimes directly anti-economic.[44] Graeber argues that much of the work performed at offices every day is either superfluous busyness—like the writing of pointless management reports and "box ticking" tasks—or anti-humanitarian, harmful "goon" work, such as forms of litigation and commercial efforts to manipulate people into buying things they do not truly need. Perhaps the most remarkable finding from Graeber's research is that many of these pointless jobs pay very well, and that, conversely, "the more one's work benefits others, the less one tends to be paid for it."[45] If janitors or elementary school teachers do not show up for work, the immediate negative results are apparent. On the other hand, if certain highly paid administrative jobs go unfilled, no

---

[44] See David Graeber, *Bullshit Jobs* (New York: Simon & Schuster, 2018), 62. These jobs may be directly anti-economic if they contribute to resource-destroying phenomena like climate change or war, while offering no tangible benefits to society.

[45] Graeber, 212.

one notices. Many of the latter jobs pay several times what the former jobs pay.[46] Graeber's research shows that the workers who hold these administrative tasks usually know their jobs are meaningless, leading to acute "spiritual violence."[47]

A key point of Graeber's analysis is that these superfluous forms of modern "labor" are not simply a product of government bureaucracy, as is sometimes assumed by libertarians and other free-market apologists. Although communist regimes have famously created nonsense jobs as part of a policy of full employment, Graeber shows that the free market also tends to create these types of jobs, especially in large corporations. There are hosts of reasons for the proliferation of unnecessary jobs in free-market economies that Graeber analyzes, including the dark sides of market competition (for example, you can win a market share both by making better products and by destroying your competition). But the biggest driver of such jobs, according to Graeber, is what he identifies as a near universal fetishizing of "job creation" as the ultimate political and economic boon, which results in feudal tendencies to create staffing far larger than necessary.[48] Graeber argues that the

---

[46] Of course, there are some highly paid jobs that are also immensely valuable, such as medical jobs. But as Graeber points out, these are the exceptions, rather than the rule. Also, they may be significantly outweighed by types of employment that researchers have argued are not only "bullshit" but are positively harmful to human well-being, such as many financial workers, advertising executives, and sundry litigators. Graeber cites research arguing that many workers in these professions destroy many times the value they take in the form of wages from the economy. Among the most persuasive of these studies is Eilis Lawlor, Helen Kersley, and Susan Steed, *A Bit Rich: Calculating the Value to Society of Different Professions* (London: New Economics Foundation, 2009).

[47] Graeber points out that many people who occupy these useless jobs (even if they are highly paid) suffer from depression and anxiety if they know their work contributes nothing to human well-being. Graeber theorizes that this is due to the fact that the charade of "work for the sake of work" violates the fundamental sense of human purpose in life. See Graeber, *Bullshit Jobs,* 113–21.

[48] See Graeber, 157.

only way to curtail the emergence of more of these pointless and soul-destroying types of jobs in the future is UBI, because it would enable people to have more free choice in pursuing the careers they find to be meaningful.

Naturally, some have disputed Graeber's statistics, and others have argued that possibly some of the jobs Graeber describes as "bullshit" could be necessary in an unknown way—though this explanation creates a further epistemic problem. Whether Graeber's account of the current job market is entirely correct is beyond the scope of our analysis here. For the purposes of my argument, it is only necessary to admit that the phenomenon he describes—pointless jobs in a free-market economy—*does* occur, and that it will likely become far more common (and soul destroying) if our economies become more efficient in the future. As Rutger Bregman observes, "As long as we continue to be obsessed with work, work, and more work (even as useful activities are further automated or outsourced), the number of superfluous jobs will only continue to grow."[49] In a world where only 20 percent of human time and effort are needed to maintain alimentary sufficiency, an insistence on work as a requirement for stable living could result in a dystopia where most of us are coerced into doing fatuous, pointless tasks, when we could be doing better things like perceiving the beauty of creation. UBI could help to prevent this.

The argument for UBI seems convincing, at least from an abstract ethical standpoint. Why, then, would anyone oppose it? Many of those who argue against UBI in the present political discourse do so for practical reasons, particularly technicalities of expense and application. These problems may be real and challenging. Nevertheless, because we are only examining the *ethical* legitimacy of UBI (not its immediate application to the present), it is interesting to consider the deeper ethical reasons why UBI proposals are commonly denigrated (usually by the political right) or ignored (by the left). In 2016, the *Economist*

---

[49] Bregman, *Utopia for Realists,* 164–65.

published a brief, dismissive article on UBI proposals, outlining the sundry risks associated with them. As any reader of the *Economist* knows, this publication tends to favor hard-nosed data over ethical trumpeting. Nevertheless, such data-focused reasoning can disguise ethical motivations that furtively pop through the lines. Such ethical motivations appeared in the middle of the article with the claim that "universal basic income would also destroy the conditionality on which modern welfare states are built."[50] The conditionality referenced here is the fundamental idea that benefits from the collective largesse should always coincide with work. This conditionality asserts that access to life without work is therefore unethical. This basic argument rests entirely on the work=life equation, and thus is opposed to the ethics of inoperativity we have explored.

The same foundational argument against UBI is even more visible in Oren Cass's invective against the policy in the *National Review.* Cass writes that UBI violates a "crucial" principle of the modern capitalist world, that is, "if you are able to work, you should work." Cass admits that technological change has (and likely will) make vast amounts of alimentary work disappear, but he argues that "when prior technological revolutions made farm and then factory labor obsolete, people continued to find new and productive vocations. More than four in five employees now work in the service sector." Cass never asks whether this shift to service-sector work is a good thing, because his basic premise is that "work not only gives meaning but provides structure and stability to life."[51] The claim that meaning, structure, and stability in life are all derived from work is another way of affirming the work=life equation.

At a core level, Cass and others who oppose UBI want to prevent the vice of sloth. Such concern is noble; no one would

---

[50] "Basically Flawed," *The Economist,* June 4, 2016.

[51] Oren Cass, "Why a Universal Basic Income Is a Terrible Idea," *National Review,* June 15, 2016.

like the government to subsidize personal laxity. However, ethical criticisms of UBI fail to realize the two different understandings of sloth that we evaluated in this chapter. The modern American popular definition of sloth equates life with work, and therefore protests against any reduction in the amount of labor humans should do, because the entire category of labor as productivity gives meaning to life. By contrast, Aquinas and others in the Christian tradition define sloth not as cessation of productivity but as lack of charity. A slothful society, on this definition, might be one in which humans work vigorously, but do so mainly for selfish, predatory, or competitive ends, or simply because they have been forced into working positions by the manipulation of those in power. Similarly, a non-slothful society might be one in which humans work less, but work out of concern for their communities and others in dependent relations or out of a desire to uncover and augment the beauty of creation.

Thus, Cass's claim regarding the innate value of work (that it provides meaning, structure, and stability) *could* be consistent with the work ethics we have charted in this chapter, if we understand the work he describes as motivated and legitimized by charity. But it seems hard to explain how forcing large sectors of the population into low-paying service industries or pointless jobs in order to survive is consistent with promoting charity. I do not imply that service work is itself demeaning or uncharitable. Plenty of bartenders, teachers, ride-sharing drivers, dancers, cooks, and repair persons work diligently because they appreciate their craft and wish to use it to build their communities. Great dignity resides in these jobs. The question is whether we should force people into these fields for stagnant wages as part of a campaign to keep humans working for the sake of work itself. The labor may not be demeaning, but the exploitative circumstances could be.

The example of sex work illustrates the difference between charitable and non-charitable work circumstances. Sex as a basic human activity can be motivated and consistent with charity, defined as concern for others and joy in the presence of community. However, most of us recognize that when a person is forced by poverty to have sex in exchange for money or resources, something goes awry. Those who resort to sex work because no other options allow them to survive have essentially been raped by the economy. The sex itself may be noble and good, but the circumstances create a toxic environment that eliminates whatever charity may be inherent in the sex act. The demeaning character of such work becomes amplified when we consider that sex work itself is unnecessary—no one truly *needs* to have recreational sex. Hence, forcing people to do it at the risk of destitution is exploitative.

Along the same lines, in a world where necessary work could be performed with 20 percent of human time and/or energy, maintaining a population of service workers who labor because they could not support themselves without doing unnecessary tasks would constitute exploitation—a type of rapist economy. Only pompous paeans to the "dignity" and "meaning" of work can disguise this fact. Such paeans, of course, are rooted in a *homo faber* anthropology that affirms the life=work equation, which the ethics of religious rituals claim is false.

My point here is not to argue that the ethics of inoperativity compels us to immediately set up a UBI system. Perhaps the economy of the future will provide other ways to delink life and work. Maybe humans will decide that a shorter work week, combined with higher wages, is a better option (though a preference for this option seems to imply a belief that making a living and work must still be joined). Also, I do not intend to overlook the fact that currently much of the world still exists below a point of easy alimentary subsistence and that we have much work to do to remedy this. My point is simply that a work ethic informed by ritual inoperativity justifies challenging the status quo of work as the basis of human existence, and thus to more closely align work with real life, which is charity.

Dismantling the systems that reinforce the work=life equation is only the first part of producing a truly restful economy. Beyond removing the precarious circumstances that make humans identify with their work, we must also recruit religious and mystical resources that can teach us how to truly find leisure. As Moltmann proclaimed in the 1970s, modern humans "no longer know how to do nothing."[52] If we have been taught from the cradle to the boardroom that work brings meaning to life, undermining this worldview will take more than changing our political system. Merely offering a UBI system to counter the type of chronic anxiety that plagues our current economy might only create a world in which humans throw themselves into other kinds of exploitative circumstances because they have not learned to exist outside of *homo faber* anthropology. The school of true leisure, as Pieper argued, is the feast of worship, and no policy measures can create a legitimate feast. The most we can do from a policy standpoint is clear the way for a feast, and that is what something like UBI could do.

The Future of Work

Rituals and labor ethics may appear to be disparate domains, but this chapter has revealed a close relationship between them. Whenever we observe a Sabbath, celebrate a fiesta, or pray during a vigil, we point to a vision of life that differs drastically from that fostered by our predominant work culture, in which work equals life. These rituals show us that we must redefine how we think about sloth, and undermine the principal social outcome of the work=life equation, status anxiety.

Whether increasing automation and efficiency will lead to a society that addresses the problems of precariousness and anxiety is not clear. While the structure of technological innovation

---

[52] Jürgen Moltmann, *The Theology of Play,* trans. Reinhard Ulrich (New York: Harper & Row, 1971), 9.

seems to point toward an age of Sabbath, when humans can do alimentary work only to the extent they need to, any number of setbacks could disturb this trajectory. Factors such as a world war or a mass extinction event could drastically impair our progress toward an economy of rest. Barring these factors, the most significant threat to such an economy is a work ethic in which work=life. If we cannot change this mindset, we open ourselves to the dystopian possibility that technology may lead us to an economic treadmill—increasing efficiency leading only to more work, a preposterous mind-bending situation we are possibly only beginning to see for the first time in world history. At best, such a situation would involve endless arrays of meaningless jobs done for the amusement of elites, who would use a mixture of material monopolizing and status anxiety to make us do their bidding. In other words, at one level or another, we who are not in charge of significant capital would become "prostitutes"—if we broaden this term to mean "those who are forced to work for the unnecessary pleasure of others." At worst, it could involve the creation of artificial conflicts in which humans find productive work in obliterating each other. War is, after all, the most flagrant site of meaningless diligence. The person who—filled with the joy of assiduous patriotism—works at bomb building represents the foulest denouement of a *homo faber* anthropology, in which the conviction that work=life glorifies even work that destroys life.

Prostitution, war, or Sabbath—these are our options. We have not yet fully arrived at the juncture where we must choose one of them, because there is still plenty of meaningfully productive work to do. But if we do not begin to change the self-conception that would propel us toward the first two, we run the risk of gradually and unknowingly making a choice. In fact, this may already be the case, particularly when we consider the state of our planet itself, to which we now turn.

5

Doing Nothing and Climate Change

The same techniques used to politicize coronavirus—promoting pseudoscience and fake experts, slandering the actual experts, valuing the economy over human life, even hiding or denying data to make the issue seem less urgent and less harmful than it is—have been applied to climate change for decades. Horrified, I've seen political biases drive people to reject simple facts: climate is changing, humans are responsible, the impacts are serious, and the time to act is now.

—Katharine Hayhoe, *Saving Us*

What is the value of the earth?

This is a strange question. As a species that, for the overwhelming majority of our existence, evolved to think about immediate problems close to hand, this question challenges our mental wiring. It is closely related to a question that tickles the brains of Philosophy 101 students: Why does the world exist? For many people, the question itself does not make sense. The existence and value of the world are taken for granted. Asking "why" about them is a category mistake.

Perhaps, for the majority of our human history, we could safely ignore the question of earth's value. We needed only to consider the value of individual things within the earth. A farmer as recently as the year 1700 had to decide whether chopping down a forest and replacing it with a field was a good idea, but questioning the existential value of earth itself is unlikely to have occurred to him.

Today, this question is no longer merely a brain teaser. Humans have acquired the ability to modify the earth's existence in ways never before comprehensible. We can even destroy it entirely, if we wish. The fossil-fuel industry has granted us influence over nearly every biological process on our planet, primarily through altering our atmosphere. This power perplexes us to the extent that many of us seek to deny that we have it at all. We are like toddlers holding high-powered guns, not sure whether they are real or not.

At the present moment we are pointing these guns at one another's heads. Strong scientific consensus suggests that current levels of carbon emissions will result in temperature increases with disastrous and possibly irreversible long-term effects.[1] Climate change is, of course, a global phenomenon, but it does not affect everyone equally. People living in places such as North America are unlikely to see significant problems, aside from occasional coastal relocations due to rising sea levels and somewhat unpredictable weather.[2] However, in equatorial

---

[1] For scientific assessments of the risks associated with continuing high-levels of greenhouse gas emissions, see Mario Malina et al., "What We Know: The Reality, Risks, and Response to Climate Change," AAAS Climate Science Panel, American Association for the Advancement of Science (2014): 15–16. On the potential irreversibility of these developments, see Kevin Anderson, "Climate Change Going beyond Dangerous—Brutal Numbers and Tenuous Hope," *Development Dialogue* 61 (September 2012): 29. See also Michel Le Page, "Climate Change: It's Even Worse Than We Thought," *New Scientist* (November 4, 2012).

[2] On the different impacts of climate change on different regions of the earth, see the reports collected in Mark G. New et al., *Philosophical Transactions of the Royal Society,* A 369 (2011): 1–241. See also Anders Levermann et al., "The Multimillenial Sea-Level Commitment of Global Warming," *Proceedings of the National Academy of Sciences* 110 (2013): 13748.

regions—particularly coastal, arid ones—climate change will lead to famines, increasing storms, and other natural disasters.[3] These could trigger political upheavals such as mass migration, increased class stratification, and violent conflict.[4] Sober-minded scientists disturb us with even the most conservative predictions, while recognizing that the future could be even worse than we now imagine.

The way we answer the question of the earth's value will be decisive for determining what to do in our present context. If earth is now an object under our control, we need to understand the value it has and how this value functions. In what follows we explore what resources an ethics of inoperativity provides us for answering this question. We discover that the same work=life equation that sets up the miserable work situation we analyzed in the previous chapter is also largely responsible for many of the difficulties we face in confronting our ecological crisis. Our investigation proceeds in three steps. First, we will find that our fundamental belief that human value is measured by work causes us to assume that earth's value lies in being worked on as well. Second, we will see that correcting this assumption must lead to a change in how we conduct ecological activism. Finally, we will entertain the possibility that our response to climate change must take the form of something like a climate Sabbath, in which we give humans the opportunity to rest with the earth.

---

[3] For vivid accounts of the disastrous outcomes of these impacts, see Elizabeth Austin, *Treading on Thin Air: Atmospheric Physics, Forensic Meteorology, and Climate Change: How Weather Shapes Our Everyday Lives* (New York: Pegasus Books, 2016).

[4] These inevitably tragic political outcomes of climate change have been documented by many scientists. See especially Gar Lipow, *Solving the Climate Crisis through Social Change: Public Investment in Social Prosperity to Cool a Fevered Planet* (Santa Barbara, CA: Praeger, 2012). On the particular problem of migration as a result of population displacement, see Melissa Fleming, "Climate Change Could Become the Biggest Driver of Displacement: UNHCR Chief," UNHCR (December 16, 2009).

The Earth Is Not for Work

Halting the devastation of our earth is not easy for a host of complicated political reasons.[5] Anyone who proposes a few-step solution is culpably oversimplifying. Nevertheless, it is also obvious that the basic political problems lurking behind climate change, such as hesitance to accept popular suspicion of renewable energy sources, clinginess to old-fashioned industries, nationalistic egoism, and many more are rooted in deeper philosophical conceptions, falling broadly into what Pope Francis in *Laudato Si'* called "the place of human beings and of human action in the world" (no. 101).[6] In other words, what we think about our planet and its resources follows closely from what we think about ourselves.

There is no point in preaching that we must save our planet if we have defined ourselves in a way that harms the planet. If I view myself as a criminal at my core, you can tell me to not commit crimes, but I will almost certainly keep doing so.

----

[5] For an overview of the complexity behind political debates over climate change, see James Gustave Speth, *The Bridge at the End of the World: Capitalism, the Environment, and Crossing from Crisis to Sustainability* (New Haven CT: Yale University Press, 2008); Naomi Klein, *This Changes Everything: Capitalism versus the Climate* (Toronto: Alfred A. Knopf Canada, 2014).

[6] Commenting on Pope Francis's approach, Mark Shiffman observes that this obsession with using the natural world is rooted in a conception of human identity as a power holder: "The problem is not simply that the extent and scope of our power have outstripped our wisdom and virtue. The problem rather is our fundamental understanding of what the power that we are developing is, over what we develop it, and how and why we develop it. Since such power is a human attainment, and its development is a human activity, the root problem turns out to be at the same time a faulty sense of who and what we are as human beings—a faulty sense that both grounds and is reinforced by our technocratic relationship to nature." See Mark Shiffman, "The Other Seamless Garment: *Laudato Si'* on the Human Relationship to Created Nature," in *Care for the World:* Laudato Si' *and Catholic Social Thought in an Era of Climate Crisis,* ed. Frank Pasquale (New York: Cambridge University Press, 2019), 94.

Human identity and ethics feed into each other. In the previous chapter we found that a common form of human identity in the modern world equates life with work. This *homo faber* anthropology makes us portray human value as proceeding exclusively from the material manipulations we create in the world. According to the basic principles of inoperative rituals, this work=life equation is wrong. Inoperative rituals teach us that ultimate value for humans lies in rest, defined as communion with others in a state of charity.

The work=life equation—if left to run amok—could present an insurmountable obstacle to addressing climate change. It is not hard to understand why. Because humans are physical creatures, all our productive material work requires partnership with the earth. If human beings must find their ultimate fulfillment in making or producing, it seems inevitable that the natural world must constantly feed this fundamental human need. The work=life equation does not merely make ecological devastation easier; it requires it. Ceasing or cutting back on material production would—by the merits of this equation—be an antihumanitarian measure. Prominent climate scientist and activist Katharine Hayhoe argues that most forms of opposition to climate science "have nothing to do with science, and everything to do with ideology and identity."[7]

At bottom, many of us fear that changing ecological policies to prevent global warming will alter our economic roles, which for many of us are synonymous with human life itself. Prior to speaking at a major US Christian university, Hayhoe saw an online post about the event from a professor claiming that "presenting solutions to climate change is morally equivalent to abortion."[8] At first, this claim looks like classic political posturing—making an absurd statement in hopes of convincing one's

---

[7] Katharine Hayhoe, *Saving Us: A Climate Scientist's Case for Hope and Healing in a Divided World* (New York: Atria, 2021), 135.

[8] Hayhoe, 139.

partisan fanbase. After all, nothing is worse than abortion for many conservative Christians in the United States. However, upon closer inspection this claim proves to be more deeply interwoven with fundamental beliefs about the world than it might initially appear. If a basic dimension of human life is using the world's resources, deliberately using less of them would constitute something like abortion—a deliberate inhibition of the potential of human life.

On the basis of the work=life equation, efforts to stop climate change thus run against our basic sense of human dignity. This is partly why George Marshall argues that climate change is a problem we are programmed to ignore.[9] Just as UBI proposals evoke a sense of dread or dis-ease because we are terrified of the sin of sloth, climate-saving policies create a sense of *this is not who we are.* Building factories, burning coal, and driving heavy cars are activities that manifest our sense of humanity, and backing away from them makes us feel a tacit unease.

An illuminating example of this unease can be found in the "Cornwall Declaration on Environmental Stewardship," produced by the Cornwall Alliance, a group of conservative evangelical, Catholic, and Jewish leaders that denies human-produced climate change.[10] The primary thrust of the document is that human beings are valuable because of their capacity to "develop" resources and "enrich" creation. The document asserts that human beings display the image of God by being "producers."[11] Although part of the document is nobly concerned with preventing harmful outcomes for the poor that

---

[9] This plays a key part in the fascinating psychological phenomena associated with climate-change denial analyzed in George Marshall, *Don't Even Think about It: Why Our Brains Are Wired to Ignore Climate Change* (New York: Bloomsbury, 2014).

[10] See Cornwall Alliance for the Stewardship of Creation, "The Cornwall Declaration on Environmental Stewardship" (2000).

[11] See "The Cornwall Declaration on Environmental Stewardship," Concerns 1 and 2.

might result from economy-slowing ecological policies, it is clear that a key rationale behind the opposition to such policies is a motive to protect the identity of human beings as producers and modifiers of nature.

We find a marked contrast to this approach in Pope Francis's *Laudato Si'*, which does not deny the role of human beings as producers but seeks to curb a "misguided anthropocentrism" that defines human beings by technological accomplishment (nos. 115–22). The contrast between the two documents demonstrates that the pivot point in the contemporary ecology debate lies within our anthropology. Both *Laudato Si'* and the Cornwall Declaration on Environmental Stewardship rely on language and concepts drawn from Genesis, such as the idea of humans manifesting the image of God and having dominion over nature. The difference is that Pope Francis frames the identity of humans as dominion-bearing entities by the *telos* of creation noted by Moltmann and Heschel. The creation story does not end with humans having dominion over the earth and filling and subduing it. It ends with the creator entering Sabbath and thus signaling that this is what dominion is ultimately for. Although Pope Francis recognizes the value of work, he points out in *Laudato Si'* that work has lost its meaning in modern culture because of a forgetfulness of rest:

> We tend to demean contemplative rest as something unproductive and unnecessary, but this is to do away with the very thing which is most important about work: its meaning. We are called to include in our work a dimension of receptivity and gratuity, which is quite different from mere inactivity. Rather, it is another way of working, which forms part of our very essence. It protects human action from becoming empty activism; it also prevents that unfettered greed and sense of isolation which make us seek personal gain to the detriment of all else. The law of weekly rest forbade work on the seventh day, "so that

your ox and your donkey may have rest, and the son of your maidservant, and the stranger, may be refreshed" (Ex 23:12). Rest opens our eyes to the larger picture and gives us renewed sensitivity to the rights of others. (no. 237)

By calling contemplative rest "another way of working" (no. 237), Pope Francis points to the same idea Goizueta articulates when he writes that "the fiesta is, at the same time, play *and* work."[12] Goizueta's argument is that the fiesta envisions a different way to exist as a human; it is not a distraction or substitute for working life. Pope Francis also sees the ideal of Sabbath as representing more than a minor interruption in the regime of work; it is a total reevaluation of this regime. Work is only valuable as a means to rest, not the other way around.

If work does not define the value of humanity, this means that humans cannot look at the earth as reducible to fodder for work. The Genesis command to "fill the earth and subdue it" therefore has an end and a limit. An ethics of inoperativity thus values earth by Sabbath and presents earth as an element in the mutual communion of rest that is the goal of all human striving. Thus, just as we should aim at increasing rest within local communities and civilizations, we should also seek the rest of the earth. This simple idea will have enormous consequences for reframing the ecological movement.

Rest Must Define Ecological Activism

The word *activism* seems to connote aggressive work. Activists change, manipulate, and produce results. In the face of the terrifying crisis of climate change, many of us feel an impulse to work harder than ever to alter the course of our civilization.

---

[12] Roberto Goizueta, "Fiesta: Life in the Subjunctive," in *From the Heart of Our People: Latino/a Explorations in Catholic Systematic Theology,* ed. Orlando Espín and Miguel Díaz (Maryknoll, NY: Orbis Books, 1999), 91.

No doubt this impulse is good. We need robust activism now more than any other time in earth's history to alter our destructive course. We also need enormous amounts of physical labor to overhaul our infrastructure and create a new green economy. The next few decades could be among the busiest in our planet's history. The problem is that if we neglect to highlight the importance of rest as the end goal of both humanity and the earth, we may find ourselves struggling against a formidable foe: our own sense of identity. We will fix small problems and create more efficiencies in specific areas, but our *homo faber* impulse to build and change the planet may create new forms of earth exploitation.

This may sound like a dire, cynical prophecy rooted in romantic fatalism. On the contrary, it follows from simple logic; that is, efficiency, by definition, means less work. This is why, as economists such as Jeremy Rifkin have pointed out, technological efficiency platforms go hand in hand with the green revolution. Writing about futuristic scenarios made possible by digital connections, Rifkin makes a bold (perhaps overstated) prediction:

> The marginal cost of some goods and services in this green digital economy will even approach zero, forcing a fundamental change in the capitalist system. In economic theory, we are taught that the optimum market is one in which businesses sell at marginal cost. Businesses are encouraged to introduce new technologies and other efficiencies that can reduce the marginal cost of producing and distributing their goods and services, enabling them to sell at a cheaper price, win over market share, and bring back sufficient profit to their investors. However, it never occurred to economists that one day there might exist a general-purpose technology platform so hyperefficient in the production and delivery of goods and services that it plunges the marginal cost of economic activity so low

that profit margins shrink dramatically, undermining the capitalist business model.[13]

Rifkin is enormously familiar with current technologies, but his forecast may nevertheless be too heady. I do not wish to make any specific predictions of the type Rifkin makes, especially not in direct chronological terms.[14] My point is only that this scenario logically follows from the trajectory of increasing efficiency. Rifkin's reasoning regarding logistics applies to all other industries. The same technologies that make fracking and petroleum hauling unnecessary, such as wind and solar power, are astonishingly less labor intensive to maintain in good operation (unlike oil and natural gas, which only can be extracted from the ground if we use labor to procure them, the wind blows and the sun shines without our help). Another prominent example is that cargo-train transport requires far less human labor than long-haul trucking. This is why Rifkin argues that a shift from fossil fuels is inevitable—it is simply cheaper. A new renewable economy based on these types of efficient mechanisms will still need labor, but inevitably much less so.

A recognition of this fact is essential for any type of coherent approach to building a different economy, because if we insist on keeping human beings working in this new economy, we will have to invent new forms of work for them to do— what David Graeber calls "bullshit jobs"[15]—and this poses the distinct risk that these new forms of work may simply create different types of greenhouse gas emissions, or other types of ecological harm.

---

[13] Jeremy Rifkin, *The Green New Deal: Why the Fossil Fuel Civilization Will Collapse by 2028, and the Bold Economic Plan to Save Life on Earth* (New York: St. Martin's Press, 2019), 17–18.

[14] Rifkin assumes much of this will happen by the late 2020s (see the subtitle of his book). Such a prediction may be premature.

[15] David Graeber, *Bullshit Jobs* (New York: Simon & Schuster, 2018).

It is not hard to think of conceivable examples of this situation. Consider geoengineering. Utilizing particles such as sulfur or reflective mirrors could be one way in which humans maintain their drive to work more while creating "sustainable" economies, thus creating further problems. Scientists do not know the full impact of geoengineering proposals, but they caution that a quick adaptation of geoengineering techniques could result in sizable errors that could produce new forms of pollutants.[16] Geoengineering measures that involve emitting under-analyzed substances into our atmosphere could solve our climate problem, while simply causing another type of yet unknown problem to appear.

Even geoengineering techniques that do not appear directly risky still appear problematic when carefully analyzed. One of the most interesting geoengineering proposals to emerge in recent years is direct air capture, in which technological innovation finds ways of removing carbon from the atmosphere. As Michael Mann and Thomas Toles observe, such technology (if we could design it) would have one noticeable flaw. In attempting to remove carbon dioxide from the atmosphere, we would be "fighting the laws of thermodynamics, and that's a very expensive battle to wage. By some estimates, it would cost more than $500 per ton of carbon removed."[17] Mann and Toles go on to argue that, given the price, it is far less expensive to avoid putting the carbon dioxide into the atmosphere in the first place.

This raises a fascinating and disturbing query: Why would anyone even propose direct air capture as a policy for addressing climate change? The answer is simple: It would keep

---

[16] See, for example, A. Robock, "20 Reasons Why Geoengineering May Be a Bad Idea," *Bulletin of Atomic Scientists* 64 (2008): 14–18. See also the expansive discussion of the potential problems of geoengineering in Michael E. Mann and Tom Toles, *The Madhouse Effect: How Climate Change Denial Is Threatening Our Planet, Destroying Our Politics, and Driving Us Crazy* (New York: Columbia University Press, 2016), 117–30.

[17] Mann and Toles, 126.

people working. If direct air capture enables us to stay reliant on some fossil fuels while still lowering levels of greenhouse gases, we could avoid stranded carbon assets and keep our economies buzzing. Such an approach would directly increase the labor involved in producing whatever industrial outputs are created through fossil fuels and thus would create green jobs while preserving the carbon-emitting ones that currently exist. For every person employed in industries emitting greenhouse gases, there would be another person employed in industries sucking them up (the ratio may not be one to one, but the point should be clear). Energy historian Vaclav Smil points out that any carbon-capture technology that has a chance of making a meaningful difference would require us "to create an entirely new worldwide absorption-gathering-compression-transportation-storage industry whose annual throughput would have to be about 70 percent larger than the annual volume now handled by the global crude oil industry."[18] We might never find a more quintessential example of a pointless economic treadmill than this.

One hopes that the proponents of direct-air-capture research do not envision their policy as a replacement for reductions in carbon emissions but rather as a supplement to such measures. (I charitably assume that every researcher in this field would agree with this.) If so, any right-minded ecological activist would support such research at a basic level. My point is not that geoengineering is inherently bad; if it can be shown to be safe and reliable, we should applaud it.[19] In our current crisis we need every possible solution we can find. Rather, I am arguing that our fear of unemployment may create a type of pro-technological Luddism, in which we exercise

---

[18] Vaclav Smil, "Global Energy: The Latest Infatuations," *American Scientist* 99 (May 2011): 212.

[19] For example, Katherine Hayhoe describes some types of carbon-capture technologies such as "biochar" that dramatically increase efficiency by providing fertilizers for crops. See Hayhoe, *Saving Us,* 179.

absurd measures to keep people working even when it would be cheaper to support displaced workers with something like UBI while giving them the freedom to educate themselves for other projects.

The possibility of such a dystopian scenario becomes more realistic when we examine many of the factors that slow our response to climate change. When we read accounts of the possibilities of renewable energy technologies, a sense of frustration arises: Why are we failing to embrace sensible automation faster? Why are we still building highly inefficient single-family houses in sprawling, remote suburbs—without solar panels? Why are we investing in the maintenance of dirty coal energy when we know that a switch to renewables is possible? Could the answer be that we know such changes might reduce the number of jobs needed, and we do not want to face a world in which people do not need to work as much?

A modest answer could be that indeed our collective work=life equation could be (partly at least) the root cause of our foot dragging. A quick glance at popular debates over climate change shows that concerns over job losses are often the trump card for those who wish to deny any efforts to address climate change. For example, the policy group America Rising Advanced Research, which opposes the American policy proposal known as the Green New Deal, has set up an entire website that provides statistics on how many jobs will be lost by implementation of climate-change mitigation strategies.[20] The fascinating element of this rhetorical device is that it focuses primarily on only one argument against the Green New Deal: the preservation of employment. America Rising Advanced Research assumes that any reader who visits its website and sees "job loss" as a consequence of climate-change mitigation

---

[20] America Rising Advanced Research, "Green New Deal Stats," www.greennewdealstats.com. It should be noted that the source for these statistics is API, which represents America's gas and oil industries.

policies will need no more convincing to oppose those policies. This focus on job loss as the chief reason why we should not implement a carbon tax or even introduce green technologies that could compete with fossil fuels reveals the central problem: Many of us do not want to imagine a future with fewer jobs. The job has become the sacred icon of the modern world, a fundamental value that must never be touched.

I must be clear. We can affirm that the Green New Deal will create more jobs than it eliminates when combined with funding for retraining. Sound research demonstrates this with ease.[21] The problem with the more-jobs rhetoric is that it effectively buys into a logic according to which the job is the measure of human value. It also overlooks the fact that our new efficient economy will at some future point also be less labor intensive, almost by definition. The major jobs that the green revolution will create, such as retrofitting buildings for new heating and refrigeration systems, will likely be temporary (the number of old buildings is finite). At a certain point, if we truly do become more efficient, a green economy must involve less work. Climate activists should not sugarcoat this with incessant talk of "creating more green jobs." According to the ethics of inoperativity, there is nothing wrong with fewer jobs. Working less is part of the sabbatical logic of human history, grounded in God's restful image.

We must also use rest-oriented activism to address one of the most challenging problems climate activists face: consumerism. Perhaps the darkest and most depressing reality of our ecological crisis is that Say's Law is partly responsible for climate change. As technological production has become more efficient, our cultural economic milieu has simultaneously ramped up demand for more new goods to keep jobs in place, a phenomenon

---

[21] For an overview of why and how the Green New Deal will create jobs, see Marilyn A. Brown and Majid Ahmadi, "Would a Green New Deal Add or Kill Jobs?" *Scientific American* (December 17, 2019).

John Barry calls "running to stand still."[22] The consequence is that the regions of the modern world with the most efficient economies (particularly the United States) are also among the most wasteful and riddled with unnecessary commodities, many of which are toxic to our planet. Researchers have long noted that if the rest of the world were to attempt to live the way Americans do, the ecological results would be more than cataclysmic.[23] "The United States accounts for only about five percent of global population, but is responsible for 30 percent of global energy use and 28 percent of carbon emissions."[24] The reason for these shocking statistics is simple: Americans consume prolifically.

Being "anti-consumerism" is hardly new in Christian ethics.[25] Theologians and preachers often rant against the consumption habits of the West, but without carefully considering what drives them or providing only a shallow analysis of their foundations. We assume that the consumerist ethic propels itself by a desire for luxurious pleasure, or hedonism. The word *consumerist* conjures up images of laxity and repose—a wealthy businessperson lounging on a million-dollar yacht. But even abstract analysis reveals this assumption to be at least partly false. Ask any yacht owner, and you will discover that owning and operating a yacht is a boatload of work—exciting and rewarding, perhaps, but work nonetheless. Furthermore, many

---

[22] See John Barry, "Climate Change, the 'Cancer Stage of Capitalism,' and the Return of Limits of Growth," in *Climate Change and the Crisis of Capitalism,* ed. Mark Pelling, David Manuel-Navarrete, and Michael Redclift (New York: Routledge, 2012), 137.

[23] For a synthesis of research demonstrating this point, see Paul G. Harris, *What's Wrong with Climate Politics, and How to Fix It* (Cambridge, MA: Polity Press, 2013), 104–15.

[24] Environmental and Energy Study Institute (EESI), "U.S. Leads in Greenhouse Gas Reductions, But Some States Are Falling Behind" (May 27, 2018).

[25] For an overview of critiques of consumerism in Christian ethics, see Kenneth R. Himes, "Consumerism and Christian Ethics," *Theological Studies* 68 (2007), 132–53.

rich Americans with luxury items such as private gyms and vacation homes spend enormous amounts of money maintaining these possessions while not using them frequently. They are difficult to manage and often require hiring outside labor. Why do they exist? Most of us know the standard answer. Yachts, fancy cars, and mansions are largely status symbols—they exist to proclaim the elevated virtue of their owner.

If consumerism is about status symbols, we must ask a crucial follow-up question: What is the quality of the status behind the status symbols? In other words, what do the status-bearing persons wish to communicate about themselves? Recall Veblen's analysis of so-called leisure items—they are not desired because the leisure itself is valuable, but because they signal success at predatory work. Those who flaunt a mansion or a yacht (in a capitalist economy) justify their status by an appeal to labor—they have worked hard at dominating their economic sphere, using their genius to expropriate the labor of others, and thus they must manifest luxurious icons of their labor. It is all the more fitting if these icons themselves involve intensive labor to maintain.

Yachts and fancy sportscars are relatively uncommon, and thus not good examples of popular consumerist "labor icons" that affect our ecosystems. A better example of such an icon is also probably the most widespread consumerist status symbol in America: the suburban (or even urban) lawn. What is the point of a green lawn that stretches across rolling expanses in front of a home? No one will dispute that a perfectly manicured lawn is beautiful and contributes aesthetic value to the property. Also, some lawns are used for games or playing with children or pets. But these uses cannot justify the existence of lawns, because other environments for homes could be just as good for child and pet recreation and could be just as aesthetic, if well designed and maintained. The truth is that most lawns exist entirely as symbols of upper-class work status. Historian Virginia Scott Jenkins, in *The Lawn: A History of an American*

Obsession, chronicles how rising middle-class Americans produced large pieces of grass-covered property (some obscenely
large) to model themselves on how posh European aristocrats
lived.[26] Such lawns have conquered not only the American suburban landscape, but also government property and university
campuses. During the twentieth century, as lawns became more
widespread, the meaning of the lawn symbol changed. Because
Americans in the mid-twentieth century valued industrial work
over everything else (and historic European aristocrats were
known primarily as managerial or leisure workers), the lawn
morphed into a weird amalgam of aristocracy and blue-collar
diligence, a symbol of the quintessential virtuous American
laborer, who dutifully cultivated it on weekends or after work,
mowing, weeding, and fertilizing it.

Does maintaining a lawn provide pleasure or luxury to most
lawn owners? Certainly to some it does, though conversations
I have had with such people indicate they would usually prefer
that the time they spent on their lawns could be devoted to more
aesthetic and rewarding types of gardening (like growing veg-
etables, trees, and bushes). Based on the anecdotal evidence I
have received, homeowners associations usually are responsible
for mandating that lawns exist in suburban neighborhoods and
that these lawns must be maintained. This suggests that for
many, the lawn is simply a means to chores. It exists to prove
that the residents of the home situated on the lawn work hard.
Even if the residents themselves do not take care of the lawn,
they must at least pay others to do so, thus creating work and
demonstrating predatory ability. Jenkins's research provides
abundant evidence that by the middle of the twentieth century,
lawn care in the United States had become a public test of a

---

[26] According to Jenkins, "Front lawns at the end of the nineteenth century
were cultivated by the wealthy and the small, new middle class that emulated
them. . . . They showed that the homeowner was well-to-do and aesthetically
advanced." See Virginia Scott Jenkins, *The Lawn: A History of an American
Obsession* (Washington DC: Smithsonian Institution Press, 1994), 32.

citizen's work ethic.[27] Furthermore, the lawn-care industry furnishes a plethora of jobs in designing and manufacturing seeds, fertilizers, and sundry tools. Lawns exist for work.

Also, it should go without saying to any well-read ecological activist that lawns are terrible for the environment, not only because of their impact on carbon emissions, but also because of water pollution, soil toxicity, the reduction of biodiversity, and a host of other reasons.[28] By contrast, urban and suburban forests would both be less difficult to maintain and far more ecologically sustainable.[29]

The point of this excursus on lawns is to show that consumerism is not always or even primarily driven by laziness or sedentary pleasure seeking, but by the exact opposite: the work=life equation. Lawns are only one small example of this. If we look carefully at the myriad types of truly unnecessary consumer spending in the Western world, we find that most of it consists in obtaining useless status symbols that exist to prove how diligent their owners are or have been while on the path to predatory dominance. Fashion, home maintenance, and culinary trends each provide manifestations of this. Even fast food—that supposed hallmark of American laziness—does not represent a desire for luxury and convenience so much as an ability to spend less time preparing food so that we can

---

[27] According to Jenkins, articles in popular mid-century American magazines stated that "lawn mowing was the 'one act by which America judges the moral fitness of her citizens'" (Jenkins, 130).

[28] This noncontroversial observation first came to the public consciousness with Rachel Carson, *Silent Spring* (Boston: Houghton-Mifflin, 1962). Carson focused primarily on the use of toxic pesticides in lawn care, but recent research has shown that lawns also constitute a deleterious substitute for natural environments, particularly with reference to carbon sequestration. See J. William Thompson and Kim Sorvig, *Sustainable Landscape Construction: A Guide to Green Building Outdoors* (Washington DC: Island Press, 2000).

[29] Jill Jonnes points out that trees in public spaces are perhaps one of the easiest types of green infrastructure we can create. See Jill Jonnes, *Urban Forests: A Natural History of Trees and People in the American Cityscape* (New York: Viking Press, 2016), xix.

maintain a focus on our "real" work—whatever happens at the office or other work facility. Perhaps the most crystallized example of a work status symbol or labor icon consumerism is in the fitness industry, where we find unnecessarily muscled and lean bodies glorified, even though, paradoxically, the modern alimentary economy requires less muscle-based labor than ever before in history. The fitness world wants us to look like we dig up and carry rocks like medieval peasants, and run up mountains pursuing deer like hunter-gatherers, while our real jobs require us to sit at desks all day and commute to work in vehicles. We must both work and "work out." Not surprisingly, these overwhelming consumeristic obligations often conflict with each other.

If we want to reverse consumerism and its catastrophic implications for climate change, we must refrain from preaching against laziness or pleasure seeking and rather castigate the robust diligence—the work=life equation—that feeds consumerism. This will mean creating a culture of rest, one that opposes not only the preposterous emphasis on finding more jobs, but also the insistence that one should try to fashion oneself as a constant worker and thus adopt luscious accoutrements of labor.

Implementing a restful vision into ecological activism will also mean making Sabbath and vigil a vital part of what ecology means at its most basic level, which leads us to our third and final point.

We Must Give Earth a Sabbath

Giving Sabbath rest to earth may sound like romantic ethical imperative with no real-world traction. This would certainly be true if giving earth a Sabbath simply meant telling people to do fewer ecologically destructive things, and perhaps conducting a few isolated performative rituals in local communities. Such an imperative would fall into the category of what Srnicek and Williams call "folk politics"—local political actions that give participants a feeling of substantial change, but ultimately accomplish little.[30] Avoiding folk politics is the point of the paradox of inoperativity discussed in Chapter 3—rituals must not only "do nothing," but they must constitute a new form of life that affects the structural foundations of society. Although rituals lie outside the bounds of so-called normal life, they must always be what Goizueta calls "life in the subjunctive"—implying that their connection to wider forms of life is more than imaginary.

We can avoid a folk-political reduction of Sabbath if we look closely at the language of the Sabbath mandate as it is found in the earliest Sabbath traditions. In the Christian and Jewish Bible, Sabbath is not simply taking time to rest. It is fundamentally an act of giving rest to others. To be responsible for "giving" something means to be in a position with power and resources. We find this hierarchical element of Sabbath displayed clearly in the biblical commands regarding Sabbath in Exodus 20:8–11 and Deuteronomy 5:13–15. The latter of these tells the people of Israel that on seventh day "you shall not do any work, either you or your son or your daughter or your ox or your donkey or any work animal, or the resident alien within your gates, so that your male and female slave may rest as you do." When I read this passage with my students, I usually ask them what the wording of the command indicates about the type of persons to whom it was addressed. After a brief pause, most of them immediately notice the obvious qualifications of the text's audience: rich agrarian estate managers. The Sabbath command is not addressed to everyone. Sabbath observance is a mandate to patriarchs with families, livestock, agricultural technology (presumably), and servants or slaves. In other words, it is a command to those in power.

---

[30] See Nick Srnicek and Alex Williams, *Inventing the Future: Postcapitalism and a World without Work* (London: Verso, 2016), 10–11.

If you lack power, you cannot be responsible for giving rest to anyone or anything. On the other hand, if you do have a monopoly on power and you simply rest on your own in a cliquish celebrative community, your rest does not provoke real change in the world. Your Sabbath collapses into folk politics at best.

Such a collapse explains many of the failing aspects of contemporary ecological activism. For example, consider the noble-yet-ineffectual slow food and locavore movements. The idea that humans should eat locally sourced, sustainably processed food is both laudable and necessary for addressing climate change. The problem is, as Carl Honore points out, that "few of us have the time, money, energy, or discipline to be a model Slow Foodie."[31] Imagine a family sitting down at a table to eat nutritious, locally grown, climate-friendly, home-cooked food. What is the likely socioeconomic status of this family? If your answer is "rich or upper-middle class," you are probably right, and there is a good reason for that. Our current economy makes it difficult for lower-class persons to eat healthy, sustainable food for two interrelated reasons: First, the poorer you are, the less economic security you have, and the less appealing ecological purchases seem. For example, on my most recent trip to the grocery store I had to ask myself whether spending an extra few dollars on local asparagus was worth it when I may face eviction from my apartment after my current adjunct teaching contract ends. Second, sustainable eating takes time that poorer people often do not have, because our work=life equation tells us that we do not deserve to "make it" financially unless we have dedicated ourselves to working at our careers nearly nonstop.

My point is that giving earth a Sabbath must not mean constructing elitist symbolic rituals that fail to strike at the core of our current ecological predicament. It will certainly involve

---

[31] Carl Honore, *In Praise of Slow: Challenging the Cult of Speed* (New York: HarperCollins, 2005), 84.

parochial rituals, but these rituals must promote the awareness that the meaning of Sabbath, fiesta, or vigil greatly exceeds the momentary impact on consciousness that they provide. This means that ritual observers should constantly seek to make the inoperativity of their rituals seep out into the rest of their lives and those of members of their communities.

How could this happen? Before examining a possible application, let us take another glance at the ritual of the weekly Sabbath. Today, this ritual certainly does not mean what it meant when it was first formulated in ancient Israel. For ancient agrarian communities daily work most likely appeared absolutely necessary except in rare circumstances of abundance. Without refrigeration, automated water supplies, efficient energy-transfer systems, rapid supply logistics, and the myriad other forms of efficiency we take for granted today, the idea that everyone (even the slaves!) should rest for one day out of seven must have appeared absurd, even utopian. In an ancient agrarian society with relatively little agricultural technology and widespread instability, landowners would seek to make tenants and other workers labor as much as possible—anything less would result in a diminution of the landowners' political power.[32] We know this also because critics of Sabbath thought it promoted laziness, or what we would probably call "lower-class entitlement" today. For example, the Roman historian Tacitus, writing in the second-century CE, expressed what was probably a common view of Sabbath-keeping when he condescendingly described the Jews as a people who observed the Sabbath out of the "charm of indolence."[33] A major motivation for this critique was certainly anti-Semitism, but there was also a practical angle behind it. Modern readers of Exodus 20 and Deuteronomy 5

---

[32] See the depiction of the labor economy in ancient Palestine provided by Gildas Hamel, "Poverty and Charity," in *The Oxford Handbook of Jewish Daily Life in Palestine,* ed. Catherine Hezser (New York: Oxford University Press, 2010), 308–22.

[33] See Tacitus, *The Histories,* 5:4.

usually assume that it would have been easy for ancient people to take one day off, because we have become accustomed to the five day workweek. We forget that for ancient economies, allowing workers to rest for one day out of seven would have directly implied supporting these individuals through some type of wealth redistribution or, at the very least, paying them a wage that would allow them to rest during this time. Sabbath meant forcing powerful people to give up maximal productivity in favor of creating rest.

Sabbath was thus not a private, personal practice, or one that was irrelevant to the other six days of the week. It was a dramatic disruption of the economic and ecological assumptions that would have been considered common sense for ancient economies. It was a type of cessation of control—a provision of freedom in the face of scarcity. It was a demand that everyone be free from alimentary labor for a regulated period of time. On this note, I might cautiously suggest that if we want to bring the Sabbath into the twenty-first century in an authentic way, we should probably request that it last longer than one day, because our societies have become vastly more efficient than those of the year 500 BCE. I will return to this point in the following chapter.

How would this model of Sabbath practice influence the way we think about a Sabbath of the earth? Such a Sabbath would constitute a dramatic reduction in the demands we (those in power) place upon the economy as a whole, especially those who work at its lowest levels. A Sabbath of the earth is not wealthy people engaging in symbolic acts of climate-friendly elitism. Rather, it is extending to everyone the ability to use less of earth's declining resources. The extent of Sabbath can be directly measured by the level of ecological power it delivers to those who own the least.

What does this mean in practical terms? Immediately we find a connection to the UBI discussed in the previous chapter. UBI constitutes a form of earth Sabbath because it provides a level of security that enables people to think freely about the impact of their consumption on the environment. Without some level of basic alimentary guarantee, insecurity leads to a type of desperation that precludes ecological consciousness. At a fundamental level, no one thinks about climate change when living paycheck to paycheck. Especially in the "developed" Western world, forced scarcity is the best way to curtail any type of meaningful ecological movement. Members of a freezing family will burn boards from their own house to sustain life as long as possible, if no other options are given to them.

UBI or other security-producing measures will be vital for making the ecological movement meaningful for scores of people who should care about it, but often find it distant from the demands of their own survival. In part, this is due to the fact that a restless world—one without guarantees of stability—does not appear to be a space that needs preservation. During my time volunteering as a homeless advocate/ally in Chicago, I experienced a profound sense of cognitive dissonance contemplating the problem of global warming while simultaneously trying to help Chicagoans who were at risk of hypothermia while sleeping in tents in sub-zero temperatures. Of course I knew that cold winters in Chicago do not imply that global warming is not a problem—that paradox was not the source of the dissonance. Rather, it seemed absurd to think that we should be concerned with rising global temperatures when we cannot guarantee all currently existing humans basic shelter and subsistence. The reality of homeless persons sleeping on the sidewalk underneath million-dollar penthouses (some of them unoccupied and still heated) created a nearly unconquerable *weltschmerz* that made climate change seem like an irrelevant issue, even though I knew at an intellectual level that climate change itself will create the equivalent of millions of homeless persons. Extreme alimentary insecurity juxtaposed with lavish opulence undermines our ability to conceive of the planet as a humanitarian space, and it makes ecological movements appear to be one more brand of "champagne socialism." In other words, the prevalence of homelessness makes the planet seem less like our common home.

An ethical Sabbath for the earth will thus begin by giving people the legitimate potential to escape the consumerist demands of the current economy—to see the world as a restful home in need of preservation. Sabbath is *rest giving.*

Beyond UBI, what practical measures emerge from this type of sabbatical ethic? Let us consider another example: Transportation. As many climate scientists have noted, one of the most unsustainable features of modern industrialized regions of the world is the practice of single-occupancy-vehicle commuting. A report by the University of Washington, for example, found that 45 percent of carbon emissions in the state of Washington were caused by transportation, and that a reduction of only 6 percent in the rate of single-occupancy commuting could play a major role in reducing overall carbon emissions.[34]

The primary problem with single-occupancy-vehicle commuting is that it is extraordinarily inefficient. Anyone standing on a bridge over a crowded highway in the United States could marvel at the profound waste inherent in this form of human movement. Many of the vehicles are spacious yet carry only one or two people; they are powered by massive engines (often much heavier and more powerful than necessary). The need for space between discrete vehicles creates traffic jams, commuting stress, and injuries and fatalities. Why would humans do this to themselves? As Jeremy Rifkin has explained, current customs of locomotion in the "developed" world did not have to be what they are—with gargantuan freeways, sprawling suburbs, and the assumption that everyone must drive to go anywhere. These systems are the product of intentional design. Rifkin explains that from the beginning until the middle of the twentieth

---

[34] University of Washington, "Sustainability Action Plan: Update, Fiscal Year 2022 (1 July 2021–30 June 2022)."

century, "inner-city trolley systems and public bus systems were often scuttled to ensure exclusivity for automobile transport."[35]

Why did we design our infrastructure this way? It might be tempting to claim that the culture of single-occupancy commuting is rooted in laziness. The stereotype of the ignorant American buffoon who drives to the store a few blocks down the street because he is too sluggish to walk falls into line with this assumption. Ecological activists who take up this ethical explanation could resort to preaching against the luxurious habits of vehicle drivers in the United States.

However, the analysis of consumerism above should cause us to reject this answer and look again at what (literally) drives this problem. Why have we created a cultural and even epistemic situation in which we see cars as our fundamental means of movement rather than supporting policies that would provide efficient, easy-to-use public transportation? As you might expect from the arguments I have advanced thus far, I suggest that the culture of single-occupancy commuting emerges straightforwardly from the worship of work (especially individualized labor) and the matrix of status anxiety that enshrouds it. In the United States, automobile ownership and driving are hallmarks of a mindset that glamorizes labor and the management of labor. For many Americans, buying a car is a form of initiation into adult life that signals one's participation in the workforce and the ability to take care of oneself. Auto ownership is also connected to concepts of masculinity. The ability to purchase a robust car or truck and keep it in running order is a signal that one is a "real man" whose employment credentials are unquestionable. As a cisgendered male adult who does not own an automobile myself, I often experience embarrassment when I must tell people prior to work meetings or friendly gatherings that I will be taking the bus or subway or riding my clunky bicycle. When I visit family members in the historically

---

[35] Rifkin, *The Green New Deal,* 148.

automobile-focused state of Michigan, I am often asked, "So, when are you getting a car?" as if it is a crucial step in maturity I have somehow missed.

Like the expansive suburban lawn, the automobile labor icon also produces labor. In this respect, both lawns and automobiles are secular forms of the religious emblems of transubstantiation—they create the substance of the reality that they symbolize. According to a report by Brandon Gaille, the automobile repair industry alone in the United States has an estimated worth of $880 billion annually.[36] In addition to the direct physical labor involved in maintaining a vehicle, one must add the labor of highway construction, car-part manufacturing, car washes, fueling stations, advertising for cars and car parts, consulting expertise for purchasing a car, driver training, and the entire financial industry based on managing loans for car ownership. Finally, one must not forget that the fast-food industry relies extensively on drive-throughs as a source of revenue, because many people purchase fast food in order to eat while driving to and from work.

In simple terms, if we all started living closer to our jobs and using public transportation or bicycles to commute, a throng of workers visible to the heavens would be out of work. A sizable number of new jobs would be created to build and maintain public transport (and bicycles), but the most elementary mathematical assessment shows that these jobs would not come close to substituting for the behemoth workforce automobiles currently require.

What should we do about this? Making cars more efficient (by investing in electric vehicle engineering) is a small and necessary step for limiting the damage of single-occupancy commuting, but it is probably not enough. Should we launch an anti-consumerist campaign against car commuters? Certainly

---

[36] See Brandon Gaille Small Business and Marketing Advice, "31 Auto Repair Industry Statistics and Trends" (May 22, 2017).

not. A Sabbath of the earth does not command us to attack or attempt to disenfranchise the practice of single-occupancy commuting or the auto industry. Aside from being impractical and unpopular, such an antagonistic approach would remove the livelihoods of millions of people. The state of our infrastructure and zoning policies have created a world in which it is impossible for many poor people to live close to their jobs or food sources. Saying "stop single-occupancy commuting" is not an option.

Remember that the Sabbath command in the Bible does not tell slaves they must rest; it tells slave owners they must let slaves rest. The ethics of the earth Sabbath compel us to create a structural situation in which people do not *need* to drive. This would necessitate combining UBI with widespread investments in developing public transportation and infrastructure that is not only cheaper, but faster and easier to use than single-occupancy vehicles. We certainly do not lack the technology to do this. As I write, engineers at several US corporations (most prominently Tesla) claim to be on the verge of designing AI-operated, self-driving vehicles that are safer than human-operated ones. So far they have not succeeded, but it should go without saying that if we can even attempt to design self-driving cars, creating an effective public transportation system should be relatively easier. The breathtaking wealth of digital computing power developed in the last three decades is more than sufficient—even for suburbs and rural areas. The real challenge is not creating more technology, but rather building a culture that sees less labor as intrinsically good, combined with an ethical impulse to create restful situations for the poorest and most vulnerable members of our communities. This is why religious communities must directly apply the ethics of their inoperative rituals (like Sabbath) to the problem of transportation in the modern world.

The application of public transportation I have offered here is only one possible way we can give an earth-Sabbath logic to our current ecological crisis. A careful analysis would show that our valorization of the work=life equation lies at the root of numerous other unsustainable practices in other industries, such as housing, which I have hinted at above.[37] I also have no space here to show how the entire system of higher education (and the question of who and what should be educated) is deeply rooted in a non-sabbatical ethic, and that this directly impedes efforts to combat climate change.[38] The relevance of a sabbatical ideal for addressing ecological issues inherent in so-called third-world development is another area beyond the constraints of this chapter. For example, as Lisa Palmer has shown, the prioritizing of work at the expense of education (particularly for women) is a major cause of unsustainable agricultural practices in parts of Africa directly affected by climate change.[39] These subjects will require treatment elsewhere.

A Return to Earth's Value

Let us return to the question posed at the beginning of this chapter: What is the value of the earth—specifically in light of the overwhelming crisis of climate change? According to the ethics of inoperative rituals, earth's value does not emerge from

---

[37] It seems clear that the zoning policies and housing regulations in the United States are directly calibrated to create more labor for developers and homeowners and to reinforce the commuting culture I have discussed here. These same policies (such as single-family zoning) are also obviously toxic for climate change.

[38] The simple idea that education should be practical—meaning enabling one to get a high-paying job—causes universities to increasingly neglect the study of anything that does not immediately provide a marketable skill. Turning universities into large trade schools leads to a reduced emphasis on courses such as general education science—in which students might learn about the reality of climate change. Humanities courses, which are needed to change a culture obsessed with creating jobs at any cost, may be neglected even more.

[39] Lisa Palmer, *Hot, Hungry Planet: The Fight to Stop a Global Food Crisis in the Face of Climate Change* (New York: St. Martin's Press, 2017), 19–41.

the work humans do to it, because human value also does not emerge from work. Like humans, earth is for rest. This means that we must inject an ethos of rest both into our ecological activism and our search for sound policies that will address climate change. I have suggested a few preliminary ways to do this.

The reader may have been shocked that I would describe public policies like UBI and effective public transportation as potential Sabbaths. Many traditional communities see their rituals as locally confined endeavors, the sacrality of which is dependent on being separate from the world and the bustle of everyday life. But if the arguments of the first three chapters of this book are correct, and inoperative rituals point to an ultimate form of human existence, we cannot confine them to a nonpublic dimension. The bounds of sacrality in these rituals exceed what happens in church or synagogue communities. Just as telling a fifth-century BCE patriarch in Palestine that he must let his slaves rest one day a week would have massive economic and ecological implications, bringing real Sabbath into the twenty-first century will do the same.

But what about the old-fashioned rituals themselves? Do they still have value? I think they do, and in the concluding chapter I provide a few reflections on what that value could be.

Conclusion

Praying and Resting in an Overworked World

Depending on your religious perspective, the ethical ideas in the previous chapters may either invigorate or depress you, or both. Deeply traditional religious observers may be excited to learn that their most fundamental rituals like vigils and Sabbaths hold immense potential for altering the way we approach vital issues like work ethics and ecology. If the arguments of this book prove anything, it should be that ancient rituals are hardly irrelevant to modern life.

Alternatively, it might be disconcerting to realize that the rituals themselves are only valuable when they become a form of life—observing them in a rote, isolated fashion will never suffice. We must not only pray, but we must create political systems that treat humans as prayerful (inoperative) beings. We must not only keep Sabbath, but we must create economies imbued with a sabbatical ethos.

But most of us are not politicians or economists. We may have little or no influence on whether our governments institute UBI or provide efficient public transportation. We pray, go to vigils, celebrate fiestas, and keep Sabbaths the way we have for generations, and we might wonder whether these individual acts can still be meaningful. How can we do these rituals of inoperativity in a way that is ethically conscious? I offer here a few suggestions in line with some of the ideas developed in this book.

Resist Ritual Privatization

Out of (noble) concern to avoid foisting religious practices on others, it has become de rigueur to keep one's traditional rituals covert in secular modern society. The absurd paradox is that, coinciding with this privatization of ancient rituals, other forms of politico-religious acts such as the enforcement of national borders and the labor icon consumerist rituals of the marketplace have become ever more prominent. We feel compelled to share our purchases with the public, becoming prolific evangelists for our chosen brands, but we must keep our prayers and Sabbaths to ourselves.

In the social-media age, perhaps nothing could be more liberating than to see pointless, intrinsically beautiful rituals displayed in the same manner as the latest shoes and expensive beverages. Remember: consumer status symbols represent work—they are rooted in a *homo faber* anthropology. The best means to resist the hegemony of consumer religion is to offer an alternative. Like Daniel praying before an open window (Dan 6:10), we should expose our rituals of inoperativity to the world, demonstrating our faith that production does not define our value.

Deprivatizing these rituals must be done with caution, however. We must constantly keep in mind the paradox of inoperativity—if we do it merely for a purpose, it loses its value, yet we still must do it with a consciousness of its implications. Maintaining this tension can be tricky, but it is possible. During my time as a graduate student in Chicago I frequently spent Sundays with a homeless church that met under a bridge in a public park. Part of what drew me to this community was the sheer authenticity of its members and their liturgy. After experiencing years of unimaginable hardship, including vicious bullying by police and others, they were under no illusions about their political power. Their worship was also shameless and unadorned. They gained no explicit social status from singing raucously under the bridge, and no one would argue that their liturgy attained stylistic majesty. In Goizueta's analysis, their worship was praxis, not poiesis. They preached, prayed, and ate together because they were human and craved transcendence just as much as anyone else. From a productive angle, their worship did nothing.

But it also did something. It created connection and community. It fostered an awareness among themselves that they deserved recognition of their humanity. It gave them a brief respite from police harassment. It also changed my own attitude toward homelessness and the moral status of persons occupying that position in society. When you have heard people pray—perhaps while wearing oversized camo coats—you can no longer see them as nuisances or a "societal problem." The impression of their humanity becomes indelible.

The worship of the Chicago homeless community is not propaganda, but it is not private either. It represents the quest of marginalized persons to exist, to "be a people." This is what all ethical inoperative rituals should represent. If such rituals demonstrate our most fundamental human identity, they must erode the public/private binary we have constructed between categories of religious behaviors.

Embrace Inclusivity in Rituals

This principle follows naturally from the one above. If inoperative rituals depict the *telos* of human existence, they can find their highest manifestation in communal celebration—and the modern world is a global community. Worshipping communities need to structure their worship so that it invites collaboration.

Such a need for collaboration does not dictate that everyone must do the same rituals. Recall one of Rav Kook's key arguments for the *heter mekhira:* it would draw Jews and non-Jews into a mutually beneficial relationship in which non-Jews profited economically by helping Jews to partially observe the ritual of *shmita.* This type of collaboration did not imply ritual uniformity or proselytizing, but unity with difference. Kook framed this collaboration as part of the essential purpose of the ritual itself. Because inoperativity consists in a rejection (or rather transcendence) of a means-end rationale for understanding human existence, inoperative rituals must not aim at conquering, manipulating, or controlling members of other religious groups. The proper denouement of ritual inoperativity would rather be enthusiastic support for the inoperativity of others, however that may look across traditions.

I have observed this type of enthusiastic support emerge organically within diverse communities at one of the universities at which I teach. Several religious clubs at Loyola University Chicago find ways to support each other's rituals. For example, the university's Hindu Student Association has often joined with the local Hillel International chapter (a Jewish student group) to celebrate any overlapping holidays by sharing food in common festivities, such as their Kosher Holi Shabbat gathering. Muslim and Christian groups have often joined in these celebrations as well. What I have found most exhilarating about these student initiatives is that they do not minimize or sideline the religious distinctives of each community. Instead, they endeavor to "play up" each other's traditions, allowing their own peculiarities to draw them together.

Part of the reason ritual collaboration is vital in the modern world is that problems of overwork do not discriminate among religions and ethnicities. Global warming is no respecter of persons. The zealous work=life equation created by *homo faber* anthropology strives to force us all to bow unanimously before its sovereignty, and thus it makes sense that we should collectively support one another in finding ways to resist it. This is the basis for the Green Sabbath Project, an initiative that aims at helping all religious communities find ways in which their religious rituals involve giving earth a rest. The project's website alludes to the ecological potential of rituals ranging from the fishing rest days of Fante communities in Ghana to the Vrata fasting days in some Hindu groups. The point is not that these different rituals are the same, but rather that they uphold the same humanity and concern for the earth that their practitioners all possess. This is the type of interreligious collaboration that we need if we wish to preserve leisure in our instrumentalized, overheated world.

Challenge the Traditional Boundaries of Rituals

We have already established this point in Chapter 3 as the basis for the wide-ranging ethical applications found in Chapters 4 and 5. If inoperative rituals establish human identity, they cannot remain within their official borders. They point to a form of life that causes them to seep into every domain of human endeavor.

Still, it makes sense to say something about how the discrete rituals themselves can be performed with an awareness that their borders are porous. In some cases, as with Kook's approach to *shmita,* this can involve suspending aspects of the ritual in order to allow its true nature to emerge. For example, among Sabbath-keeping communities, observers could use Sabbath time to bring climate-friendly, healthful food to homeless or low-income communities whose diets might otherwise consist of heavily processed foods. In cities, rest-giving could involve providing public transportation passes to those who need them. Volunteer groups could assist in "greening" houses in older neighborhoods by installing solar panels and adding insulation. Other volunteers could refurbish bicycles to provide for lower-income individuals who might want to use this supremely ecologically efficient mode of transportation but do not have the finances to acquire them.[1] This would be work, in the traditional sense, but it would also be inoperativity, because it would constitute recognition of the intrinsic value of human beings. As in Rav Kook's understanding of the *heter mekhira,* these methods would recognize the soul of the ritual—the type of humanity the ritual creates.

Expanding the boundaries of rituals might also involve a more literal type of expansion: broadening the temporal impact of the inoperative ritual. In a simple, literal way this could mean upending the hegemony of the five-day, forty-hour workweek. As I mentioned in the previous chapter, the ancient Sabbath comprised one-seventh of human time during a period when alimentary economies were far less efficient than they are now. In ancient Palestine—and for much of human history in most places—regular caloric deficiencies and famines were ever-present threats to the working classes. "Give us this day our daily bread" for the poor implied working for whatever one needed, as frequently as it was needed. It would have seemed revolutionary to insist that one day every week should be completely nonproductive for everyone.

Today, in a world with astonishing economic efficiency, the only way to continue that revolutionary quality of Sabbath is to broaden it even more, compelling us to consider whether our workweeks should be perhaps far shorter than five eight-hour days, which is a legacy of 1920s Fordist industrialism. In 1930, John Maynard Keynes observed the increasing level of technological wizardry (which was a far cry from what we have now) and speculated that within several decades workers would only

---

[1] In my experience working with homeless persons in Chicago, I have noticed that there are many individuals who would like bicycles for transportation but are unable to afford them. A further structural problem that compounds this issue is the absence of bike lanes on most urban roads. Part of healing the earth could involve advocating for increased bicycle accessibility in these areas.

need to labor for fifteen hours a week.[2] Keynes was obviously wrong in his prediction, but several economists have argued that he did not have to be. The consensus among economic historians and current theorists seems to be that Keynes was right about the technological possibilities of the future, but that he failed to recognize the deeply entrenched cultural patterns that would force people to keep working even when alimentary sufficiency had been reached.[3] These cultural patterns, as I have argued, are rooted in the life=work equation. Part of the way religious observers of rituals such as Sabbath can destabilize this equation is by making Sabbath (or any other type of in-operativity) take up more of life. Practitioners and clergy can emphasize that the qualities of Sabbath time—appreciation of beauty and reduction of status anxiety—should characterize more than just one day out of seven.

Another way to ensure that rituals seep outside their institutional boundaries is to continue the ancient legacy of prophetic critique. Figures such as Isaiah and Amos continually reminded worshipping communities that unless rituals such as sacrifices and festivals create a merciful form of life, those rituals are not only worthless, they are dangerous (see Am 5:20–24; Isa 1:11–17). The danger lies in the fact that worship without justice—faux inoperativity—not only ignores but openly mocks the humanity of those who lack the resources to live with dignity. The bold ability of the prophets to recognize these failures of their own worship is still vital today, particularly to bring about the "messianic" type of inoperativity we found in Agamben's work. This type of genuine ritual inoperativity can only emerge when rituals do not mechanize human life, but liberate it.

---

[2] John Maynard Keynes, "Economic Possibilities for Our Grandchildren," in John Maynard Keynes, *Essays in Persuasion,* 358–73 (New York: W. W. Norton, 1963).

[3] For an overview of recent reevaluations of Keynes's prediction, see Lorenzo Pechi and Gustavo Piga, *Revisiting Keynes: Economic Possibilities for Our Grandchildren* (Cambridge, MA: MIT Press, 2010).

Prophetic critique of rituals does not need to be strident or aggressive. The best example of the legacy of prophetic critique applied to rituals in recent years was perhaps an event that occurred during Pope Francis's 2015 visit to Mexico, during which he celebrated a mass at the US/Mexico border, on the Mexican side. In one sense the pope's act of worshipping on the border was a regular, inoperative act of appreciating divine beauty. But in another way it was a self-reflective critique of the ritual, a prophetic interrogation. By celebrating the one body of Christ in a space of bodily separation, where humans are forcibly categorized into separate groups with separate rights, the pope tacitly raised the question of how one can practice communion in an anti-communicative political situation. Effectively, the ritual proclaimed: "This is supposed to be communion. But full communion is not happening here." By pointing to its own inadequacy, the pope's ritual exploded the boundaries of what some might assume worship is "for." His act remained a form of genuinely pointless leisure (in Pieper's sense), while simultaneously making a point—a perfect example of the paradox of inoperativity analyzed in Chapter 3. Using prophetic critique to maintain this paradox is key for allowing inoperative rituals to expand beyond their borders.

Finally, not all clergy and congregants have the opportunity to celebrate an inoperative ritual with such trenchant effectiveness as Pope Francis did. Nevertheless, every religious leader or practitioner has the opportunity and the obligation to understand fully the impact and societal meaning of the inoperativity within rituals. During my time as a minister I sometimes celebrated communion with congregants by adding into the homily the words "this is an incomplete process." No full communion exists until all can eat. No full Sabbath happens until all can rest.

That is why the most vital ethical element in rituals should be hope. Faced with the cataclysmic potential of climate change and the grinding, soul-crushing force of work-related status anxiety, it may be tempting to write off rituals as mindless rigmarole. The assumption that rituals can quickly become perfunctory and ethically inert is not without basis. Nevertheless, if we understand rituals as a form of life—an end in itself that also forecasts our ultimate state as human beings—they can foster genuine conviction that a better world is possible. This better world would be one in which humans view productivity not as the purpose of their existence but as a means to finding that purpose. It would be a world where the word *leisure* does not immediately conjure up images of lavish vacations and myriad entertainments, but rather points to the essence of charity, the recognition of the beauty of creation in all persons. Although this world appears foreign and distant in our present context, the legacy of vigils, fiestas, and Sabbaths tells us that it is far closer than we think. Sabbath, according to Heschel, is the existence of God, represented by the rabbis as a bride, eager for celebration. We need only welcome her.

Acknowledgments

Given my wide-ranging adroitness in the realm of doing nothing, many people merit gratitude when I do something such as write a book. First, I am forever indebted to the wisdom and guidance of my mentor and favorite theologian Miguel H. Díaz, without whose intellectual wizardry this book would never have come to fruition. Crucial also were the astute insights and criticisms from Colby Dickinson and Devorah Schoenfeld, who both mercifully boosted me over the many hurdles that appeared in the research process.

While writing I also reaped insights from numerous scholars at Loyola University Chicago, especially Joshua King, Molly Greening, and Cathy Buescher, who provided research-related pointers for several chapters in this book. Additionally, I found ideas and encouragement from other thinkers such as Emily Cain, Hille Haker, Paul Adaja, Meghan Toomey, Shane Gormley, Martin Tomszak, Kathleen McNutt, Teresa Calpino, John Diamond, Sarah Tarkany, Matthew Kemp, Jonathan Hatter, Dannis Matteson, and Jacob Torbeck. While working at Loyola I have deeply appreciated the institutional support of Robert Di Vito, Bret Lewis, Michael Patrick Murphy, Mara Brecht, and Joanne Brandstrader. I am eternally grateful for the overflowing generosity of Christopher Skinner, both intellectually and materially. Others also deserve thanks, but they are too many to name here.

The kindness and competence of Robert Ellsberg, Jill O'Brien, and others at Orbis Books were essential, as was the direct assistance of Jon Sweeney—a brilliant writer who also edited the manuscript. All remaining errors are exclusively mine.

Finally, if the indomitable Jeri Tocco had not cheered me on and patiently tolerated my rants and ramblings, I would have accomplished nothing.

Index